SAUL
KING OF
ISRAEL

SAUL
KING OF ISRAEL

By VICTOR S. STARBUCK

Chapel Hill · THE UNIVERSITY
OF NORTH CAROLINA PRESS
1938

COPYRIGHT, 1938, BY
THE UNIVERSITY OF NORTH CAROLINA PRESS

Van Rees Press · *New York*

CONTENTS

Saul's Hunting, 1

Atarah, 17

Jabesh Gilead, 38

The Philistines, 56

Michmash, 76

Amalek, 108

David, 131

Goliath, 146

Adullam, 174

Abigail, 204

Ziklag, 230

Gilboa, 257

SAUL KING OF ISRAEL

Saul's Hunting

I

So the girls of Benjamin
　Sang in dances long ago,
In the morning of the earth,
Danced and sang in festal mirth
When they brought the vintage in,
　Set the baskets row on row—
How young Saul, the tall and brown,
Seeking asses, found a crown.

II

Saul the son of Kish is gone
　Hunting Kish's asses,
Rising in the hush of dawn,
While the early dew is strawn
　On the cobwebbed grasses.

He is tall as heart could wish:
　Maidens when they meet him
Smile upon the son of Kish,
　Bow their heads to greet him.

First is he in every race,
　In the wrestling strongest;
He is swiftest in the chase,
Slings his stone to farthest place,
　Draws his arrow longest.

SAUL'S HUNTING

With him goes a shepherd lad,
    Bondman of his mother,
Jethir, of the Tribe of Gad,
    Servant, friend, and brother.

Through the greening vales they go
    Where young buds are peeping,
Up the slopes where myrtles grow,
Over heights where melting snow
    Sets the brooks a-leaping.

All the world is glad with Spring,
    Sweet with thorn-trees blooming;
Everywhere are birds a-wing,
And the reedy fenlands ring
    With the bittern's booming.

On and onward still they fare
    Through the shining weather,
Breathing deep the fragrant air,
Blithe and strong and debonair—
    Two young lads together.

Through Shalisha's pleasant wood,
    Over Ephraim's passes,
Finding that the earth is good,
Glad of life and hardihood—
    Heedless of the asses;

Drinking of the darting brook,
    Munching bread of barley,
Sleeping in some rocky nook,
    Up at morning early.

Kish hath ploughing to be done,
    Wood to cut for burning—
Here is cloud and wind and sun,
Shady rest where wild brooks run,
    Country lore for learning:

SAUL'S HUNTING

How the locusts march in bands
    Like a mailed battalion,
On what crags the ibex stands,
How the ostrich spurns the sands
    Swifter than a stallion.

Yet the hottest hearts will slack,
    Swiftest feet will tire,
Bread grow scant in haversack—
Boyish minds at length turn back
    Toward tent and evening fire.

They were in the Land of Zuph
    On the third day's morning:
Saul exclaimed, "It is enough!
We have eaten all our stuff—
    Let us be returning.

"Can we live like swine on roots?
    And belike my father
Hath forgot these straying brutes
    Caring for us rather."

Then the servant answered, "Here,
    In the village yonder,
Dwelleth Samuel the Seer:
God hath whispered in his ear
    Words to make men wonder.

"Let us haste and seek him out
    Ere the daylight passes.
He can tell us, never doubt,
    Where to find the asses."

So they rested on a bed
    Sweet with grass, and ferny,
While the sun was overhead;
Searched their bags for crumbs of bread;
    Then resumed their journey

SAUL'S HUNTING

    Moving slowly Prophet-ward
      Through the scanty tillage,
    Till the field-path, trodden hard,
    Wound across an olive-yard.
      Maidens from the village

    Came to draw, at eventide,
      Each with jar on shoulder.
    One was fair and starry-eyed,
    One was bosomed deep and wide,
      And the third was older:

    Drab Hadassah, auburn-tressed,
      Caring but for duty;
    Dark Ahinoam, deep of breast;
    Atarah, the loveliest,
      Like a rose in beauty.

    So they met the strangers there
      Whispering olives under;
    Drew their veils o'er face and hair
    (Two were young and one was fair)
      Less in fear than wonder.

    Then said Saul, "From Benjamin
      Come we, asses seeking.
    Is the Man of God within?
    May we to his presence win?
      May we hear him speaking?"

    And Hadassah answered, "Yea;
      Hearest thou not the shouting?
    Seek the Seer without delay.
    Whatsoever he shall say
      Trust his word, undoubting."

SAUL'S HUNTING

Then Ahinoam answered, "Lo,
   From the High Place rising,
See the smoke ascending slow,
And the people, where they go
   To the sacrificing.

"Samuel the ram will slay,
   And on altar bind him;
For we have a feast to-day.
Tarry not, and in the way
   Ye shall surely find him."

Atarah stood still, apart,
   Gave no word of greeting;
Yet Saul felt his pulses start,
And her heart, as his own heart,
   In his bosom beating.

Thanks he gave, and up the knoll
   Took the path assigned him;
But he felt the damsel's soul,
That it left her flesh, and stole
   On silent feet behind him.

III

Samuel, the Man of God, was gray and old
   And sore at heart, and tired.
He felt the people's love for him grown cold;
   Knew they desired

A king to rule them, be their shield and sun,
   Lead forth their bands in war:
He saw the wreck of all that he had done
   And striven for.

SAUL'S HUNTING

For he had put God first in everything,
    And had been well content
To labor that the Lord might reign as King:
    Now he was spent;

Like some gaunt beast, too old to drag the plough,
    Turned out to live or die,
To gnaw scant herbage from a broken bough
    Withered and dry.

And he had judged the people forty years
    Through peril and distress.
His eye was hard, but in his heart were tears
    And bitterness.

The sons he loved had turned aside for bribes,
    Like Eli's sons before:
He knew men hissed their names through all the tribes—
    Each had his whore.

And he had pleaded with them many days,
    Had threatened and implored:
They used his power, but walked not in his ways,
    Served not his Lord.

And still there echoed through his memory
    A warning unforgot:
"Because his sons have made them vile, and he
    Restrained them not."

And how the tidings came that in the strife
    Was lost the Ark of God;
And Eli fell and died, and Phinehas' wife
    Cried, "Ichabod!"

Yea, even so the glory must depart
    From him, and from his house—
A tree that sin had rotted at the heart,
    With withering boughs.

SAUL'S HUNTING

And yet, they might have waited till he died
  Before they made a king,
Stripped off his honors, flung him thus aside,
  A broken thing.

But God had said to him, "It is not thou:
  It is of Me they tire.
They have rejected Me; yet give them now
  What they desire.

"Yet show them how their king will take away
  Their sons, their land, their seed;
And when they cry against him in that day,
  I will not heed."

And God had said to him but yesterday,
  "To-morrow I will bring
A man who seeks for asses gone astray:
  Anoint him king."

So Samuel waited patiently, but none
  Had come to ask of him
For asses, and the day was all but done;
  The dusk grew dim.

Yet, tarrying still, he watched the people going
  Up to the sacrifice;
He heard the Levites' silver trumpets blowing
  Against the skies.

Once this had broken from his heart the fetter
  And lifted it on wings;
But now he mused, "Were not obedience better
  Than offerings?

"Or what avail the timbrel and the psalter
  For souls made blind by sin—
The blood of bullocks sprinkled at the altar,
  The stench, the din?"

7

SAUL'S HUNTING

Again the trumpets blew; he heard the laughter
    And shouts from the High Place:
Like one who dreams, he followed slowly after
    With halting pace.

And through his muse, the voice of one desiring
    To find the Seer, began
To speak—and through his heart, like angels choiring,
    "Behold! The man!"

He thought that he should hate the Lord's anointed
    Who came to take his place;
But now he looked, and saw the man appointed:
    A boyish face

He had, as open as a wind-blown meadow
    Where fair field-lilies bloom;
A face as yet unclouded by the shadow
    Of sin and doom;

And, loving him, he felt his burden lifted
    As if by unseen hands.
Here, surely, was a youth divinely gifted
    For God's commands.

"I am the Seer," he said, with lips that trembled,
    And tears were in his eyes
He knew not why: "The people are assembled
    For sacrifice.

"The hour is at hand of the oblation,
    And ere the twilight cease
I offer, for myself and for the nation,
    The sacrifice of peace.

"But thou must lodge with me: behold, I know thee.
    Share thou my food and fire.
To-morrow, ere thou goest, I will show thee
    All thy desire.

"As for thine asses, dost thou seek them yet?
  They have been found. And see:
On whom is all the hope of Israel set,
  If not on thee?"

He spake no more, but walked, erect and tall,
  As if himself were king,
Up the steep way to the High Place. And Saul
  Followed him, wondering.

IV

So they sacrificed, and after
There was feasting, wine and laughter,
Saul, with wonder in his face,
Seated in the chiefest place
At the Man of God's right hand,
While the mighty of the land
Sat below, and gazed upon him,
Wondering at the honor done him.

Samuel bade his servant, "Bring
What I told thee to put by—
Portion worthy of a king."
And the cook brought forth the thigh,
Passed the lords and elders all,
Set it at the place of Saul;
And they filled his horn with wine,
Brought him curds in creamy clots,
Honeycomb and wafers fine,
Figs and dates and apricots.

Then said Samuel to the bidden
Guests, "Although his worth be hidden
Under guise that simple seemeth,
Here is one the Lord esteemeth,
Choosing him for mighty things;

SAUL'S HUNTING

One that shall be wise and great,
For his sword shall strike through kings;
Men shall bless him in the gate.
He shall ride and prosper still,
Doing all Jehovah's will."
And the people sat and gazed,
All bewildered and amazed.

When the feast was done, the Seer
Whispered in the stranger's ear,
"I have much to say to thee:
Come this night and lodge with me."

To the housetop went they up,
Where the air was fresh and new,
And the heaven, like a cup,
Dripped with starry light and dew.
There the Prophet spake to Saul
How the Lord was God of all,
And His power was great to wield men,
And His love was strong to shield men;
How the sun and moon and star
He had made, with none to aid;
How His hand was great in war,
Blessing spear and bow and blade;
And he urged the youth to give
All his heart to God the Holy;
Whatsoe'er befell, to live
In His service, meek and lowly.
Then he spake of dream and wonder,
Cherubim with golden lyres,
Tall archangels clothed with thunder,
Seraphim like flaming fires;
Till the stripling saw the splendor
Shine like dawn above a hill,
Knelt before him in surrender,
One with him in heart and will.

SAUL'S HUNTING

V

It was the dawning of another day
    When Saul awoke from sleep.
A dimness, neither light nor darkness, lay
    On field and steep.

His slumber had been thronged with tangled things—
    Shrill trumpets, wild alarms,
And fields where chariots rolled, and bearded kings
    Shouted in arms.

And there was one who moved through all his dream
    In quietness arrayed,
Mid cursing trumpets and the torches' gleam—
    A star-eyed maid.

And now there fluttered in his brain like birds
    The scenes of yesterday;
The olive grove, the Prophet's cryptic words,
    And through the gray

Of evening the ascending altar-smoke,
    The mallet's jarring thud
Upon the bullock's head beneath the oak,
    The spurting blood.

All these and more he strove to ravel out—
    Things done from things that seemed:
Kings, Prophet, chariots—till he lay in doubt
    If still he dreamed.

Then Samuel's voice brake through his clouded sense,
    And bade him rise, for day
Was nigh at hand, and he would send him thence
    Upon his way.

SAUL'S HUNTING

He roused the sleeping Jethir, yet bemused
   With dreams and drowsy wine,
And clinging to his couch, like one unused
   To bed so fine.

They rose and went. Day halted in the east,
   And mist was on the hill;
The village folk yet slumbered after feast;
   The ways were still.

The dews of night were on the Prophet's hair,
   And in his steady eyes
The clear, still light of peace, that comes from prayer
   And sacrifice.

The winds of night had swept his spirit clean
   Of anguish and unrest:
He had beheld the ways of God, had seen
   That they were best.

They paused without the gate. There spake the Seer,
   Leaning upon his rod,
"Let Jethir go before; for thou must hear
   The word of God."

As Jethir went, a newborn breeze of morn
   Blew o'er the misty soil;
And from his breast the Prophet took a horn,
   And poured the oil

On Saul's dew-dampened locks, and spake the word:
   "The Lord hath made thee King."
And from a thorn-bush by the way, a bird
   Began to sing.

SAUL'S HUNTING

VI

So Saul went home across the flowering land
With more in mind than he could understand.
No more he raced his friend from hill to hill,
Nor spake, but plodded onward, musing still,
Amazed with doubt. Should he indeed be king?
He, who had never thought of anything
But ploughing stony fields and tending flocks,
Or seeking hiding-places in the rocks
From roving Ammonites and Philistines
That robbed their pastures and laid waste their vines?
Or did the Prophet jest?—But he had poured
The hallowed oil, and called upon the Lord.
There was no mockery in those quiet eyes
That searched him while they blessed. There were no lies
Beneath that venerable dome of hair
On which had fallen thick the dew of prayer.

Yet how could he be king? a lad so raw
He hardly knew a sentence of the Law?
How build a kingdom from these wrangling tribes?
His very friends would answer him with gibes,
Would bring him gifts of cattle-dung and gourd,
A crown of nettles and a reed for sword,
Then roll him in the dirt—He felt his face
Flush at the thought, and strode with swifter pace.

His servant rallied him in boyish sport:
Saul frowned, and sharply cut his jesting short.
He was a lad no longer, but a man:
He needed time to organize; to plan
If he should tell his father what had passed
Between the Seer and him, or keep it fast.

They came to Rachel's tomb, and there three men
Told him the asses had been found again

SAUL'S HUNTING

And Kish was mourning for his absent son—
Even so the Seer had said. He sent them on
Before him, scarcely answering; and began
Again devising plan on shadowy plan,
How he should arm his men, how go to fight
Against Philistia or the Ammonite.

At Tabor there were three who gave him bread
And wine. He took them as the Seer had said,
And hastened onward, busy with his thought.
How might he tame the tribes? How bring to naught
Philistia's power? How from the country drive
The desert thieves? His brain droned like a hive.

Then, by the fortress of the Philistines
At Bethel, there came winding through the pines
A band of prophets, and they prophesied
With pipe and harp and psaltery. He tried
To pass them heedless; but the minstrelsy
Stirred all his blood, and would not let him be.
He turned and followed them: and now there came
God's Spirit on him like a bath of flame.
He felt a new heart throbbing in his breast,
And lo, he prophesied among the rest.
And therefore they that deal in proverbs say,
"Is Saul among the prophets?" to this day.

But now a voice was sounding in his ear:
"The Lord is with thee. Wherefore dost thou fear?
Devising vanities? Return and wait
Until God call thee, be it soon or late.
I have ordained thee king. Shall God decree
And not perform? Cease then, and let it be."
And then a peace came o'er him, sweet and fair,
As those cool drops on Samuel's silvered hair.

VII

So the maids of Benjamin
  Sang the tale in olden days
When they bore the harvest in,
  Dancing by the trodden ways
Where the barley sheaves were brought,
  Ere the harvest feast began—
How young Saul for asses sought,
  Went a lad, and came a man.

Saul, the son of Kish, is come
  Home again from straying.
Bid the voice of grief be dumb,
  Set the pipes to playing!
Kill the fatling, pour the wine,
  Knead the dough for baking,
Clothe the lad in raiment fine,
  Mirth and music making!

He told his kindred of his journeying:
  The paths in Ephraim were wild and steep;
Upon the crags were wild goats clambering,
  And all their valley-lands were white with sheep.

In Zuph, he said, they still had corn to sell,
  And there were vineyards and good meadow-ground.
The Man of God had entertained them well,
  And told them that the asses had been found.

And at the last he told them of the maid—
  The one with starry eyes, who did not speak—
That he had met beneath the olive shade;
  How she had drawn her veil across her cheek,

And yet he knew that she was fair, he said,
  And gentle, and her garments smelled of myrrh.
Did not the time draw near for him to wed?
  And would his father send and ask for her?

SAUL'S HUNTING

    But of the kingdom spake he not a word:
        His parting with the Prophet in the morn,
    The oil upon his head, the hidden bird
        That sang so sudden from the wayside thorn.

    Yet, whiles he led the flocks from glade to glade
        Or drave the furrow through the stubborn clod,
    He dreamed of kingdoms, and a star-eyed maid,
        And waited word from Samuel, and from God.

Atarah

I

The day was set for the marriage-feast;
    The guests were bidden, both kith and kin,
There was bread in store, and the fatted beast,
    And pipe and timbrel to make a din.

All Rama's damsels kept holiday-tide,
    With bangled bracelets and gem-decked hair,
And Atarah, the chosen bride,
    Was ever fairest among the fair.

For Kish to Ahimaaz had sent
    Gifts of honey and wine and bread,
Saying, "I pray thee, be content
    To give thy maid for my son to wed.

"Ask of my neighbors, and learn that Kish
    Hath sheep and asses, camels and kine,
Broad pasture-lands as the heart could wish,
    And gardens fair with olive and vine.

"And Saul is Kish's only son,
    Goodly in body, fair and tall,
Strong to labor and swift to run:
    Give thy daughter to wed with Saul."

ATARAH

Ahimaaz laughed; for he was great,
  A prince of the city of Ramathaim,
The elders bowed when he sat in the gate;
  He had broad lands and a noble name.

And Samuel, the Judge and Seer,
  Did him honor and loved him well:
Of the first of Ephraim he was peer—
  And he might be King of Israel.

Ahimaaz laughed; then blinked like a cat,
  And pursed his lips, remembering well
Saul's mighty shoulders, and how he sat
  First at the feast of Samuel.

So he bade the messengers tarry a day
  While he took counsel of friends and kin;
Then girded his loins and went his way
  And sat in the gate where the folk come in.

He sat in the gate, and his heart was proud,
  For all bent low who passed his place;
Till Samuel came, and he rose and bowed,
  Saying, "I pray thee tarry a space."

So Samuel sat; and Ahimaaz
  Spake of matters both near and wide,
With solemn "therefore," and wise "whereas,"
  And "furthermore," and "if this betide."

And Samuel listened with solemn look
  And innocent eyes that held no guile,
Though he read the man like an unrolled book,
  And knew of his purpose all the while.

Ahimaaz questioned of holy things,
  Of Ark and Altar and hallowed bread,
Of tithes and firstlings and offerings,
  And of things impure that had touched the dead;

And he spake of the Law and of politics,
  And the caravan that had come from Tyre,
Of oil and water that will not mix,
  And whether the stars were gold or fire;

He reasoned of wisdom and right and truth,
  Of late and early, of most and least;
And then he spake of the stranger youth
  Who had sat so high at the Prophet's feast:

From Issachar, was it not, he came?
  Was he held in honor among his clan?
Strange that he could not call the name—
  He seldom had seen so tall a man.

And the Seer made answer simply enough
  That the stranger came from Benjamin,
A dweller in tents, and wild and rough,
  Yet held in honor among his kin.

His father was Kish, the son of Ner,
  Owning asses, cattle, and sheep:
And men of substance his kindred were,
  With grapes to gather and fields to reap.

Then rose the Prophet, and stroked his beard:
  "Though he come of a tribe that is weak and small,
He is one that shall be both loved and feared,
  And men shall bless in the name of Saul."

Ahimaaz rose, and reverent bent,
  And the twain went each his several way;
And Ahimaaz the messengers sent
  Back to Benjamin, answering "Yea."

ATARAH

II

So Saul went up, with kin and friends beside,
To Ramathaim, to wed the starry-eyed
And slender Atarah. The promised dower
Was paid by grumbling Kish; the nuptial hour
Agreed upon; and Atarah and her maids
Would sit long days on end, their shining braids
Entwined with garlands wreathed of fragrant bloom,
The whiles they plied the distaff and the loom,
Strung pearls, compounded dulcet odors, stitched
On wedding garments blazoned and enriched
With beads of jet and scarlet broiderings;
And Atarah oft would deck her hands with rings,
Her hair with pearls, and don her bridal gown,
Then, turning on her toes and looking down,
Would smooth its folds—the others uttering cries
Of rapturous wonder, not unmixed with sighs
Of envy for the bride's unwithered bloom,
Her nuptial finery, her handsome groom:
For in the company was scarcely one
Who had not gladly wed the stalwart son
Of Kish. And then, the wedding dress put by,
The loom would clack again, the shuttle fly
Across the warp; while all kept watch for symbols
Of fortune good or ill: to drop their thimbles,
Mislay their needles, or to snarl a skein,
Were auguries of ill, and they would feign
Deep consternation, rosy fingertips
Pressed hard together, and red, pouting lips
Pursed up—and then some token of good luck
Would sweep the room with laughter: one would pluck
Her dulcimer, and all conjoin to raise
Some sweet or mocking ditty: so the days
Went by on feet of song, with happy labor,
And glad good wish, and gifts from friend and neighbor.

But God commanded Samuel, saying, "Bring
The tribes together: let them choose a king."
And Samuel sent his runners through the land
Of Israel, saying, "Hear the Lord's command:
When next the moon shall set her silver bow
In heaven, let every man of Israel go
To Mizpah, there to stand before the Lord;
For He will do according to His word
And choose a king to rule you." Then with speed
The tribes of Israel gathered in the mead
Before the watch-tower: meat was left in dish
And wine in cup; Ahimaaz and Kish
And Abner, and the men of Rama, each
Saddled his beast, and there was hurried speech
And stuffing bags with provender; the ways
Were thronged with men and hung with dusty haze,
As Israel hastened to the gathering,
Each one with hopes in heart of being king
When he returned. And Saul took leave in sorrow
Of her he should have wed the second morrow,
With pledge of swift returning, sealed the vow
With touch of burning lips on mouth and brow,
And clasped her slender hands, before he followed
Ahimaaz and Kish.

                    And Atarah swallowed
The lump that all but choked her, turned away
And hurried to her chamber, where she lay
Across her bed, and wept for girlhood's dream
So sudden broken into bits, the cream
Of life turned sour, remembering how her thread
Had snapped that day, and how the damsels said
It augured dreadful things. And now the groom
Gone on the wedding eve! What fearful doom
Might meet him by the way? For when the folk
Were thus assembled, often tumults broke

ATARAH

    Among them; and she knew her lover strong
And valiant, one that would not brook a wrong
Nor suffer insult lightly. So she kept
Her time of bitterness, and hoped and wept
And hoped again by turns; and every day
She clomb the towered gate to watch the way
From Mizpah, hoping any hour might bring
Her Saul— Nor dreamed that he should come a king.

III

All Israel was gathered in the field
   Around the watch-tower; and the Prophet stood
   Before the people, while the elderhood
Drew near to hear the will of God revealed.

And Samuel said, "Thus saith the Lord your God,
   'I brought you out of Egypt, from your hard
   And bitter bondage: it was I kept guard
Above you, I that brake the tyrant's rod.

" 'I clave the sea before you, that its waves
   Should be a wall to you on either side;
   I whelmed the hosts of Pharaoh in their pride,
And in the bubbling brine they found their graves.

" 'I led you through the desert: every dawn
   The manna fell; the water from the rock
   I gave, and sustenance for herd and flock,
And in the fiery cloud I led you on.

" 'I brought you to the land of corn and vines
   And milk and honeycomb, and gave you rest.
   I saved you from the kingdoms that oppressed—
Moab and Midian and the Philistines.'

"But ye this day reject the Lord, and fling
   Your insults in His teeth: ye disobey
   The God that saves you, saying to Him, 'Nay,
We know our mind, and we will have a king.'

"And since the Lord is gracious, He will do
   According to your asking. Let the tribes
   Draw near and stand before me, while the scribes
Observe the lot, and see that it is true."

Then came the tribes of Israel, led each one
   By chosen men of valor and renown,
   And such as fittest seemed to wear the crown,
To guide the host, and sit upon the throne.

But Saul the son of Kish had wandered far
   Without the camp, along a chattering stream
   That wound through pasture-lands, his mind adream
Of one whose eyes were like the evening star.

A drone of bees was in the quiet air;
   The water whispered o'er its rocky bed,
   Of Atarah; the swallows overhead
Sang "Atarah, Atarah, Atarah, Oh most fair."

He fell to weaving in a golden mesh
   All he had seen and known and dreamed of her:
   His meeting with her first, beneath a blur
Of twilit olive trees, and how his flesh

   Had yearned for her; and how she spake no word,
      Although her sisters chattered on like pies;
      But he had seen the radiance of her eyes,
   And known her voice a viol, though but heard

ATARAH

    In fancy. Then his father's sending men
        To ask her hand in marriage; the delay
        Of breathless waiting, and that wondrous day
    That the ambassadors had come again;

    His coming to her father's house; that first
        Sound of her voice—a little stumbling speech,
        With words like ripples lapping on a beach
    In living coolness, to assuage his thirst.

    And he had touched her hand, and felt the flood
        Of ecstasy through all his being run;
        And there had been the kiss that made them one
    To life's last hour, in soul and flesh and blood.

    And she was his—this starry loveliness
        Beyond all beauty seen or dreamed before!
        If he were king, she could not love him more;
    If he were slave, she would not love him less.

    Yea, she would be his wife, sleep by his side,
        Be mother of his children, milk his ewes.
        How fair would be her feet among the dews
    Of dawn, how sweet her voice at eventide!

    And oh, how blithely would he drive the share
        Through stony fields, how gladly would he reap
        And prune the vines, and tend upon the sheep,
    And spend a life of labor in her care!

    Yea, this were better than to be a king.
        The kings of all the earth, whoe'er they were,
        Would envy him his Atarah, lovelier
    Than stars of night or fragrant buds of Spring.

    The kingdom seemed a thing of little worth.
        Let be what would, and let the Lord decide
        According to His will. To wed his bride
    Were better than to rule the realms of earth.

ATARAH

The Prophet had ignored him: if he saw
   He had not marked, although he had a word
   Of greeting for his father, and the Lord
Ahimaaz; and Saul had watched in awe.

He had forgotten, it was clear, that long
   Hour on the housetop, and the mist-white morn
   That followed; the anointing by the thorn;
The bird that shook the flowering bush with song.

Or had this ever been? Sometimes, he knew,
   The brain will make a dream from naught, and day
   Will come with turmoils, yet the dream will stay,
And who can tell if it were false or true?

What mattered it who sat upon the throne?
   To-morrow was the day that he should wed
   The star-eyed Atarah; and he should tread
The heights of earth, and all things were his own.

Such things had never been—except in tales
   That shepherds told, nor cared if they were true,
   In golden noons, when through the breathless blue
Of heaven the clouds went by like drifting sails.

And yet, if this should be—if God should lift
   A yokel from the furrow to the crown!
   His cheek burned crimson underneath the brown
With wonder at the thought— What splendid gift

Were this for her he loved! And so he turned,
   Yet lost in musing, back to where the folk
   Milled in the meadow, and the altar-smoke
Ascended slowly, as the Levites burned

The trespass offering; and on his seat
   Of judgment sat the Prophet, while the tribes
   Drew near by heads of houses, and the scribes
Were gathered in a circle at his feet.

ATARAH

 And Saul beheld the Man of God begin
  To cast the lots: a single stone leaped out.
  As through a dream he heard the people shout,
"The lot is cast, and falls on Benjamin."

 A murmur of derisive anger swelled
  Among the thronging folk, for Benjamin
  Was least among the tribes, and for the sin
Of Gibeah, when all the tribe rebelled

Was all but blotted out. "Shall free-born men
  Bow down to one of such a tribe as this?"
  "Not wolfish Benjamin!" "He cast amiss!"
"The lot was false. Good Prophet, cast again!"

Saul stood in wonder, while from man to man
  The murmur spread; but now the lots were thrown
  Again; the rumble deepened as the stone
Leaped forth that bare the name of Matri's clan.

His tribe and clan! Again the Seer let fall
  The stones, and yet again: the house of Ner!
  The family of Kish! There was a blur
Before his eyes; he felt himself grown small

Beneath all human stature, and a ring
  Of suns spun round him. Once again the Seer
  Had cast the lot: a roar assailed his ear
Like falling waters, "Saul is chosen King!"

The thing was past believing. Tremblings ran
  Through every fiber, and a pounding tide
  Beat in his temples. Oh, that he might hide
His face from those that cried, "Behold the man

"That thinks himself a king!" The wagging head,
  The pointing finger, every taunt and jeer
  Derision knows. The baggage-train was near:
Sole place of refuge. Like a hare he fled

Among the carts and saddles, burrowing
  Mole-like beneath the bags of provender,
  While through the gathering there ran a stir
Of wonder: "Where is Saul? Where is the King?"

And there it was at length the searchers found him,
  And brought him to the Prophet, flushed as red
  As any maid, but taller by a head
Than Israel's mighty men that thronged around him.

Then Samuel said, "Behold the man, and bring
  Your praise before the Lord. For none is found
  Like God's anointed King!" And all the ground
Was shaken with a shout, "Long live the King!"

And some drew near, and proffered to obey
  The King's commandments, pledging him their vows
  Of service, while he stood with burning brows
And downcast eyes, and wist not what to say.

But others cried aloud in snarling scorn,
  "Can this man save us? Shall he have the rule
  Of Israel's mighty ones—this beardless fool
From Gibeah's wilderness; this yokel born?

"We own him not as king! By craft of hand
  Hath Samuel cast the lots, and made his choice
  Of one that like a dog will heed his voice,
And leave him still the ruler of the land."

And so the gathering ended all in rage,
  With shouts, and weapons drawn on either side,
  And oaths and turmoil, till the Prophet cried,
"Return each man unto his heritage

"Till God fulfill His purpose, and make known
  His will by signs and wonders. Ye rebel
  As did your fathers; but the Lord shall quell
Your pride, and set His King upon the throne."

ATARAH

    But Saul returned no answer, gave no sign
      That he had heard the insults and the gibes;
      But said to those that came from all the tribes,
    Whose hearts the Lord had touched, "If ye be mine,

    "Then follow me. At Gibeah is a hold,
      Though now it lies in ruin, that defied
      The hosts of Israel in their power and pride.
    We will rebuild its ramparts as of old,

    "And make a citadel that shall withstand
      Philistia, Moab, and the desert thief.
      Give me your strength of arm, your heart's belief,
    And we will make a kingdom of this land."

    So Saul and Abner set them in array;
      The trumpet sounded and the drums were heard;
      The march began; and like a soaring bird
    The heart of Saul went singing all the way.

IV

    The men of Saul are marching: the minstrels
      touch the string.
    Bow down, ye men of Israel, to God's anointed
      King!
    The men of Saul are marching; and as they
      march, they sing:

    The men of Saul are marching; and few they be,
      but bold:
    The King shall wear a scarlet robe, a diadem of
      gold.
    The men of Saul are marching, like Jephtha's
      host of old.

The men of Saul are marching: lift up the voice
    and cry,
Ye fields and every growing thing, ye hills and
    mountains high!
The men of Saul are marching— Behold the King
    pass by!

The men of Saul are marching: exult, O
    Benjamin,
Thou little tribe, thou feeble tribe, despised
    among thy kin!
The men of Saul are marching, to bring the
    kingdom in.

The men of Saul are marching: ye cymbals,
    clash amain!
Ye pipes and lutes and dulcimers, take up the
    glad refrain!
The men of Saul are marching; and Saul the King
    shall reign.

The men of Saul are marching: new hope and
    joy they bring.
Ye gates and everlasting doors, lift up your heads
    and sing!
The men of Saul are marching: Oh shout, and
    hail your King!

V

Agag of Amalek dwelt in the South:
Like a pomegranate rind was the red of his mouth.
He was fierce as a leopard and swift as a hare,
And his scimiter keen as the claw of a bear.

Agag of Amalek traded in men:
He took them in battle, and sold them again.
He bargained in infant and woman and maid,
And his white-turbaned followers throve by the trade.

ATARAH

Agag had afrits to do his behest:
They brought to him tidings where trade was the best.
Now they came to him swiftly as birds on the wing,
Saying, "Israel gathers to make them a King."

Agag of Amalek sprang to his steed,
And called to his followers, ready at need,
"Take bridle and saddle and target and spear;
The fold is unguarded— Why tarry ye here?"

The huntsmen of Amalek rode like the wind
Till the hills were around them the desert behind:
The highlands of Judah and Benjamin's borders
Lay bare and defenseless of watchmen and warders.

The raiders rode fast and the raiders rode hard,
But the women kept close, and the cities were barred;
And Agag was wroth, and his followers cursed:
They were weary with riding and burning with thirst.

The huntsmen of Amalek slackened their speed,
For faint was the horseman and foam-flecked the steed.
The dust of the road in their nostrils was dry;
The sun was a buckler of brass in the sky.

At dusk of the even, they came to a spring
Nigh unto Rama, engirt with a ring
Of whispering olives, with ferns at the brink:
They leaped from their horses and knelt there to drink.

They rubbed down their coursers, and each took a tuck
In the sash of his scimiter, cursing their luck,
And grumbling at Agag, the chieftain who led,
For their bags and their bellies were empty of bread.

And then, down the highway from Mizpah, there came
A dust-cloud, and weapons like flashes of flame,
With blowing of trumpets, and shouting amain,
"God save His anointed one! Long let him reign!"

ATARAH

Agag of Amalek sprang to his steed,
His men-stealers following— Great was the need!
And he cried from the saddle, "Strike spur for your lives!
The hornets of Jacob are out of their hives."

The gate had swung open, and forth like a dove
Atarah fluttered, to welcome her love.
And Agag of Amalek muttered, "The maid
Will sell for a price that shall pay for the raid."

Agag of Amalek, blessing his luck,
Stooped like a hawk; like a tercel he struck.
From his galloping courser bending low
He lifted the maid to his saddlebow.

The courser wheeled, the bit in his teeth;
His hoofs struck sparks from the stone beneath,
And over their horses' withers bent,
Like a flight of swallows the raiders went.

But Saul had seen, and he cried to his band,
"After the raiders with buckler and brand!
First place in the kingdom is his that shall bring
The starry-eyed Atarah back to the King."

Agag of Amalek laughed in his beard;
Fair was his captive, and little he feared.
No cloud-breasting eagle could match in his speed
The fleet-footed coursers of Amalek's breed.

The raiders of Amalek rode like the wind
Till the wastes were around them, the mountains behind.
The wind-drifted desert sand blotted their track,
And footsore and hopeless the hunters turned back.

ATARAH

VI

Rend ye your garments, raise the bitter wail,
Let every cheek be pale,
  Daughters of Rama!
Lay by the harp and lute,
Dulcimer, pipe, and flute,
And let the zither's tinkling strings be mute
  For Israel's sorrow.

Lament, tear off your jewels, make you bare
For Atarah the fair,
  The lovely virgin!
The starry-eyed and tall
Damsel, desired of all,
The well beloved and betrothed of Saul
  Is captive taken.

And ye, her father and her sisters twain,
Let fall your tears like rain
  For her dishonor.
Hadassah, auburn-tressed,
Ahinoam, deep of breast,
Agag of Amalek hath robbed your nest
  Of its fair nestling.

And thou, O Saul, our newly chosen King,
Thine hour of triumphing
  The thief hath blighted.
This day must thou lay down
The scepter and the crown,
Rend off the scarlet, gird the sackcloth brown,
  And sit in ashes.

Oh hour of anguish and of bitter grief!
Agag, the desert thief,
  Amalek's chieftain,

ATARAH

Leaned from his saddle high,
Caught her, and stilled her cry—
His turbaned horsemen, swift as eagles fly,
  Carried her captive.

They bore her far into their desert land
Of thorn and sun-bit sand,
  Treeless, unwatered.
Long shall her father wait,
Watch from the towered gate;
She comes not, though he mourn her soon and late—
  Atarah comes not.

In fury and despair did Saul the King
Follow with sword and sling
  Her ravishers:
As well might he pursue
The eagles through the blue.
He lost their track where stunted thorn-trees grew
  In shifting sand-heaps.

Hush ye the harp, nor seek to comfort him,
Daughters of Ephraim!
  There is no solace
For woe that lovers feel:
Where sorrow sets her seal,
Not song nor wine nor time itself can heal
  Such bitter anguish.

Yet needs must ye bewail her and lament,
Your heads in grief be bent,
  Ephraim's daughters!
Strip you and make you bare,
Strew ashes on your hair,
For Atarah, the starry-eyed and fair,
  Amalek's captive.

ATARAH

Oh would to God that she had died instead;
That she might make her bed
  In the cool shadows,
Laid in the quiet mould,
In peace and darkness rolled,
With all the loved and lovely ones of old
  Who rest from sorrow!

Yea, would that she in sepulchre were laid
With Jephtha's little maid
  And Deborah,
With Leah, tender-eyed,
And Achsah, Othniel's bride,
And that the dusky wings of death might hide
  Her starry beauty.

O Mother Rachel, let thy voice be heard
Like to a sorrowing bird
  Mourning in Rama,
For her, the undefiled,
Borne to the desert wild,
For Atarah, for thy beloved child,
  Because she is not!

VII

To Rama Saul returned, with dust on head.
  He yet might wear the crown,
But what is glory, when the heart is dead,
  Or honor, or renown?

Ahimaaz brake forth with grief afresh,
  Beholding his despair,
And sat with sackcloth girded on his flesh
  And ashes in his hair;

ATARAH

While all the folk of Rama kept a fast
   And mourned before the Lord
With humble hearts, till seven days had passed;
   Yet still there came no word

Of Atarah. The wastes of thorn and sand
   Had swallowed Agag's men
And her their prisoner: from that desert land
   No captive came again.

Ahimaaz, although his woe was deep,
   Of her he loved bereaved,
Yet suffered not his policy to sleep,
   And schemed the whiles he grieved.

For Atarah's loss was neither help nor cure
   Nor hope of ransoming:
And still the loss of Saul must he endure,
   The newly chosen King?

Not if his brain held wisdom, and his tongue
   Had power over speech
As in the days of old. The King was young:
   The crown was yet in reach.

With unctuous words he urged the lad to stay,
   Since they were both bereft;
And dropped insinuations, day by day,
   That he had daughters left:

Hadassah, though she passed the prime of life,
   Was faithful in her task;
Ahinoam would make a gentle wife
   If worthy man should ask.

ATARAH

He should not find another in the earth
   Like Saul, who now was grown
So great— Yet he had seen his noble worth
   When he was all unknown.

They both had griefs; but there was naught to gain
   By sorrowing overmuch
Or overlong, for things that brought but pain—
   And life was filled with such.

He hoped that Saul would wed, and have a son:
   The King must leave an heir
To take the kingdom when his life was done:
   The realm must be his care....

And so he played on Saul's embittered heart
   With skill that masked its skill,
And wrought upon him, with his crafty art,
   To win him to his will.

Saul lingered on: Ahimaaz was kind;
   Saul's sorrowing heart derived
A solace from his sorrow, and was blind
   To what the man contrived.

Sometimes he met Ahinoam, dusky-pale,
   Soft-footed, gentle, meek,
At household duties, and her lids would veil
   The pallor of her cheek.

Yet might he mark within her shadowy eyes
   A grief too great to bear,
Before her lashes fell. The maid was wise,
   Discreet, and not unfair.

And when they met in courtyard or on stair,
   She passed with simple grace:
Sometimes the sun would make her dusky hair
   A nimbus round her face....

ATARAH

Youth was not made to dwell with wintry grief:
   Love, withered at the root,
Sometimes puts forth a melancholy leaf
   That may not come to fruit.

Saul took the dark Ahinoam for bride
   To ease his sorrow's smart,
But Atarah, the lost and starry-eyed,
   Was mistress of his heart.

Jabesh Gilead

I

Who hath despised the day of little things—
The baby at the breast, the child at play,
The colt with wind-tossed mane? Who shall misprize
The lion's whelp, the eagle's young, whose wings,
Half-fledged, are yet too feeble to essay
The sun's dominions and the realms of day?
He yet shall dare the winds and mount the skies,
And swoop, with rending talons, on the prey.
The warrior armed, the lion when he cries
Full-voiced, were feeble once: now who so strong as they?

And he that builds a realm must sweat and bleed
Through days of doubt and danger, laboring long,
While frost and wrinkle mar the cheek and hair,
And all his striving brings but scanty meed:
The mighty men despise him, and the throng
Beholds unheeding; but the man grows strong
Through failure and defeat, and learns to dare,
To judge, to rule, to overcome the wrong.
And in the end shall be the trumpet's blare,
The crown of victory, the harping and the song.

The years had passed, and brought forgetfulness
That Saul was King. For Israel knew no reign
Except Philistia's—hers whose iron heel
Trampled a land that languished in distress
And impotence. Saul made but scanty gain:
One city, hemmed with hills, was his domain;

JABESH GILEAD

Two hundred men obeyed his trumpet-peal,
Withstanding, with their valor and their pain,
Dark Moab's spears and Midian's crooked steel;
But at Philistia's power they struck, yet struck in vain.

And still the sickle mowed the bearded corn,
The pitcher lipped the bubbles of the spring,
The patient oxen turned the scented loam,
And no man wist a nation had been born,
Nor any knew that Israel had a King.
The years go stumbling on; the seasons bring
Their gifts of oil and wine and honeycomb,
The vintage, with its dancers in a ring,
The time of sowing and the harvest home
And Autumn's withered leaves and April's blossoming.

The kingdom, like a marshlight seen through fogs,
Shone faint and far, and fitful as a dream;
And youths forgot to dance and maids to sing,
While men that knew no master snarled like dogs
At one another, matching scheme with scheme—
Ignoble lords, that each would be supreme
In clan or city—and the venomed sting
Of envy struck, even amid the gleam
Of hostile arms; for there was none to bring
Deliverance to the land, nor any to redeem.

But here and there were acts of wrong redressed
And captives freed, and deeds of valor done
By Saul and his: a robber overthrown,
An overweening noble that oppressed
His people brought to judgment; battles won
With raiders from the lands of sand and sun,
And weapons girded on and trumpets blown
Against Philistia; till the realm, begun
By little deeds, a crescent splendor shone,
And one great victory would make the nation one.

JABESH GILEAD

II

King Nahash of Ammon came up in his might
To Jabesh of Gilead, hot for a fight.
His warriors were many, his camels were tall;
He coiled like an asp under city and wall.
The city awoke, when the night was gone by:
The tents of the strangers stretched out to the sky.
The hosts of the desert in leaguer were set,
And Jabesh was caught like a fish in a net.

The elders of Jabesh took counsel, and knew
Their weapons were weak and their warriors were few.
They trembled in terror, they wept in their grief,
And sent men to treat with the Ammonite chief.

With dust on their heads they besought him aloud,
And the spirit of Nahash waxed haughty and proud:

"O Nahash of Ammon, thy glory is great:
Thou art couched like a leopard in highway and gate.
Our city is thine, and our cattle and wives;
Yet show us compassion, and grant us our lives.
Lo, this has been told us, both once and again:
The rulers of Ammon are merciful men.
Then make us a pact: we will serve thee as lord;
But shoot not thine arrows and draw not thy sword!"

Then Nahash gave answer, "What league may we hold
With spawn of the robbers that spoiled us of old?
And well have ye spoken, 'Our city is thine'—
From Jabbok to Bashan is Gilead mine!
For we took it of old, and we held it as prey,
And ye came like the jackals and snatched it away
When our hands were made weak by the Amorite war.
Your homage I scorn, and your league I abhor.

But now will ye serve me, ye traders in lies?
This pact will I make you: to thrust out your eyes.
For reproach unto Jacob, of robbers the chief,
I will set in your foreheads the brand of the thief!"

They wailed, "O thou Mighty One, grant us, we pray,
For glory to Ammon, a week of delay!
Let us send to our kindred, through Israel's coasts,
And tell them how proudly the Ammonite boasts.
It may be our God will raise saviour and friend—"
And Nahash, in mockery, answered them, "Send!

"Yea, send unto Reuben! He dwindles and pines,
While Moabites ravage his olives and vines.
Ask aid of Manasseh. He hides in the rocks,
And the lion of Midian plunders his flocks.
Go, cry unto Ephraim, Judah, and Dan:
The Philistines fry them like eggs in a pan.
Ye ask me for mercy, and such I bestow,
For Nahash of Ammon is merciful. Go.
Yet publish this proverb through Jacob again,
The rulers of Ammon are merciful men."

III

Then forth at speed the runners went,
With dust on head and garments rent,
In all their kindred's ears to tell
How Nahash mocked at Israel.

At Heshbon first they told the tale;
But Moab dwelt in Reuben's vale.
To Shechem they the tidings bore;
But Midian vexed Manasseh sore.
In Ephraim and Dan, the folk
Groaned hard beneath Philistia's yoke.

JABESH GILEAD

The Northern Amorites made war
With Zebulun and Issachar;
And in the South, on Simeon's neck,
Was set the heel of Amalek.
In every tribe were men dismayed,
Too dull for ruth, too weak to aid,
Though sons of those who wrenched their land
By combat from the foemen's hand.

IV

And at the last the envoys turned and went
   Despairing homeward, heavy-footed, sore
In heart and soul. Their looks were downward bent:
   They might return, and they could do no more.

There was no help for them in Israel:
   The land appeared forsaken and accursed
Of God; each village had its woes to tell,
   And yet of griefs their own seemed far the worst.

They thought of fathers they had left behind,
   Who waited for the aid that would not come;
The ox-goads sharpened and made hot to blind;
   And now they wept, and now their lips were dumb,

Remembering vineyards where, when grapes were ripe,
   The brown-armed damsels moved among the leaves,
And grassy pastures where the shepherd's pipe
   Blew softly through the dusk of Summer eves.

And all the lovely sights and sounds of home:
   The wandering flocks, the heaven-soaring lark,
The slant of sunbeams on the furrowed loam—
   And over them the dread of endless dark.

JABESH GILEAD

They would return, to share the blinding pain,
   The hopeless darkness that they could not mend—
Never again to look on sun or rain
   Or kindred faces, till the world should end.

And yet, with grieving much, they missed the way;
   For little sees the eyes that sorrow fills;
And wandered long, bewildered and astray,
   Through narrow glens, beset with scowling hills.

They found no man to tell them of the road,
   And on those rocks a goat could hardly find
A foothold; yet their sorrow, like a goad,
   Still pricked them onward; till, as day declined,

The footway opened on a narrow plain
   Hid nestlike in the endless wild and steep
Of mountains, rich with grass and fields of grain,
   And there were vineyards, and a fold for sheep.

Midway the plain, a stronghold barred the way:
   A wall-crowned hill, against the blackening sky;
And whispering at its feet, beneath the gray
   Of olive leaves, a little stream went by.

Around its spring-fed source a knot of folk
   Were gathered: ploughmen smelling of the mould,
With patient oxen standing in the yoke;
   Tall shepherd lads who led their flocks to fold;

And women bending o'er the rock-hewn pool
   To draw the water in their earthen jars;
While over all the vale there spread the cool
   Of evening, and the gleam of early stars.

JABESH GILEAD

In olden days the place had been so strong
   Its people had no fear of any foe,
Until all Israel, for a woman's wrong,
   Had taken it by craft and laid it low.

And Saul had found it but a ruinous heap
   Of fire-gnawed timbers, lime and tumbled stones,
Where conies gamboled, and the straying sheep
   Grew fat on grass that sprang from warriors' bones.

He had rebuilt the ancient fortress well—
   Beginning of the realm he hoped to make,
And made of it so strong a citadel
   As not Philistia's mighty hand could shake.

Now drew the runners near, and asked what hill
   And town was this, that had so high a wall?
And one made answer, while the rest were still,
   That this was Gibeah, the hold of Saul.

The names they knew not; but like aged men
   Who tell a tale, repeating o'er and o'er,
And wandering from the track and back again,
   To say again what they have said before,

Even so the messengers began to tell
   (Though more from sorrow than with hope of aid)
How Ammon heaped reproach on Israel
   And Nahash made the Jabeshites afraid.

And of their search for help the envoys spoke,
   And how, in every place, their errand failed.
And when they ceased from speaking, all the folk
   Of Gibeah lifted up their voice and wailed.

Then Saul came, following the oxen home,
   Bronzed, bearded, hard from labor at the plough,
His feet yet heavy with the furrow's loam,
   Dust mingled with the sweat upon his brow.

JABESH GILEAD

Now long it was since he was chosen king,
  And he had gained no kingdom in those years.
For realm, he held this valley, with its ring
  Of barrier hills; for host, two hundred spears.

At times he led them forth against the men
  Of Moab, or to wet their thirsty steel
In Midian's blood, or from his mountain den
  Struck like a viper at Philistia's heel.

But for the most he labored like an ox
  Among his fellows, swung the winnowing-fan,
Brought home the sheaves and tended on the flocks,
  The simple chieftain of a petty clan.

The dark Ahinoam had borne him sons
  And daughters, and his father was grown old:
He toiled for bread to feed his little ones,
  And fire and fleece to keep them from the cold.

And as to men whose memories are blurred
  By crowding circumstances, comes a chime
Of things in happier childhood seen or heard,
  But now half hidden by the skirts of time,

Even so to Saul the promise of the crown,
  So bright of yore, was tarnished and grown gray;
Not all forgot, nor doubted, but borne down
  Beneath the common things of every day.

And with it there was joined a memory
  So bitter-sweet it made the teardrops start—
A star-eyed maid, a whispering olive tree:
  Fair fruit of Sodom, ashes at the heart.

And so he labored, tiring flesh and bone
  With care of field and flock and herd and vine,
Lest madness steal upon him from old pain,
  And dulled his soul with toil instead of wine.

JABESH GILEAD

And now he wondered whether Jonathan
　Were come from hunting, and if he would bring
Fresh game. The lad was grown almost a man,
　Lusty and strong, and good with bow and sling—

A son to make him proud.... And then that cry
　Of lamentation made his pulses leap.
He paused, and asked of Abner who stood nigh,
　"What aileth them, that all the people weep?"

And Abner answered, in few words and sad,
　How Jabesh had been caught in Ammon's snare,
How Nahash sware to blind the men of Gad,
　And of the messengers and their despair,

And said, "Thou hast two hundred girt with sword,
　And sixty more that wield the sling and bow."
Then Jethir, pressing near him, cried, "My Lord,
　My father dwells in Jabesh. Wilt thou go?"

And Jonathan, who stood with bow in hand,
　A half-grown stag across his shoulders thrown,
Cried, "Gideon had three hundred in his band,
　But Samson slew a thousand men, alone."

Then sudden, like a warrior's hand, was laid
　God's hand upon his heart, as long ago
At Bethel; and it shook him like a blade
　Made bare for battle. "Bid the trumpet blow!

"And call my swiftest runners here," he said.
　And while the ram's horn startled hill and wood
He caught an axe and struck his oxen dead.
　Then, even as they wallowed in their blood

He hewed them piecemeal—shoulder, neck and thigh,
　Grisly, with shattered bones, besmeared with sand
And blood: and when the messengers drew nigh
　He gave the horrid collops to their hand.

JABESH GILEAD

"Take these, and speed from Heshbon unto Dan,
    And sound the trump in Israel's utmost coast,
Till ye have summoned every tribe and clan
    To come to battle with the Ammon host.

"The place of mustering is Jordan Ford.
    No man may rest, or tarry by the road.
And he that hath not javelin or sword
    Shall come with sickle, axe, or cattle-goad.

"Then show these tokens: say that I have sworn
    That even thus it shall be done, to all
The herds of him that hears the trumpet-horn
    And follows not to battle after Saul."

V

Now fast and far the tidings sped;
    From hill to hill the trumpets blew:
On all the people fell a dread
    From God, and swift to arms they flew.

They left their herds in hill and glade,
    They dropped the sickle in the field,
The plough in earth, to gird the blade,
    To take the spear and brace the shield.

But few the weapons they could boast,
    So hard Philistia wore them down:
There was no smith in all their coast,
    No armorer in any town.

Yet some indeed had ancient glaives
    And javelins, bitten deep with rust,
Hid in the fastnesses of caves,
    And targets covered thick with dust.

JABESH GILEAD

And those who had no weapons took
   The common tools that served their trade—
The iron-shod goad, the pruning hook,
   The reaper's keen and crooked blade.

At first in little furtive groups,
   Mustering by three and five and ten,
They gathered into larger troops
   In wilderness and mountain glen,

With backward glances, half afraid
   To see their tents go up in smoke,
Their herds swept off by Midian's raid,
   Their fields laid waste by Moab's stroke,

They grew a band, a host, a horde,
   Still swelling as it swept along:
Down Ephraim's eastern slope they poured,
   Three hundred thousand warriors strong;

Yet warriors of such craven moulds
   A wolf at bay had made them cower:
Philistia, from her mountain holds,
   Looked down and mocked their feeble power.

To Bezek Saul had led his band—
   Hard-bodied men, with spears and blades
Wrenched from Philistia's heavy hand
   In sudden strokes and midnight raids;

And some were armed with bronze cuirass
   From Amalek or Moab torn,
And bull-hide bucklers, bossed with brass,
   Of old by sheiks of Midian borne.

Well skilled were they in all the craft
   Of petty war their chieftain knew—
To vex the foe with stone and shaft,
   To stand, assail, retreat, pursue.

JABESH GILEAD

And there Saul met the gathering hosts,
   Mustered, and set them in array,
Appointing captains to their posts
   To lead them on the battle day.

Yet oh! to lead a thousand men
   As valiant as his chosen band,
And send these cravens home again,
   Who feared their shadows on the sand!

And when the evening hour came in,
   Then Samuel the libations poured,
Burned offerings for the people's sin,
   And asked the counsel of the Lord:

"Wilt thou go with us to the fight
   And victory give, or shall we fail?"
God answered, "Go ye up and smite.
   Draw forth the sword: ye shall prevail."

Saul sent the Gaddite runners back:
   "Look ye that Nahash hear it not,
But swords to aid ye shall not lack
   To-morrow, ere the sun be hot."

They went at speed. Then Saul arose
   And moved his host across the stream:
Pale moonlight shone on spears and bows;
   The flood sent back a watery gleam.

Even here had Jephtha crossed the ford
   To Gilead in the days of old,
And put to flight the desert horde—
   The minstrels still his triumph told.

On Jordan's eastern bank again
   Saul in three bands his host arrayed:
Abner should take a thousand men
   Well armed with buckler and with blade,

JABESH GILEAD

Two hundred thousand more with goads
   And axes, and should march a course
To occupy the southern roads
   Toward Rabbah and the Jabbok's source.

The King himself would northward lead
   A chosen band, with spear and targe,
And make his way through wood and reed
   Toward Jabesh, by the Yabis' marge,

And close beside the Ammon camp
   Lie ambushed till the east grew pale;
Then, while the mist lay thick and damp,
   With furious charge the foe assail.

To Jonathan he gave the rest,
   Bowmen and slingers, tall and brown,
To skirt the camp from north and west
   And take the hills above the town.

Now takes each band its several road
   Through Gilead's hills and pastures dry;
And Jordan, rippling swift and broad,
   Gives back again the unshadowed sky.

VI

Nahash came, the King of Ammon, with his host
   against the land,
And his sword was like the lightning, and his
   spear was in his hand.
Those that followed him were many as the stars
   in Summer sky,
And their hoofbeats like sea-thunder when the
   surf is rolling high.
Like a flood they compassed Jabesh, beat its gates
   and lapped its wall—
But they dreaded not Jehovah, and they
   reckoned not with Saul.

JABESH GILEAD

When the elders of the city sent men forth to
    pray his grace,
Nahash' heart grew high and haughty, and he
    mocked them to the face:
"Send, and cry for aid to Reuben, Judah,
    Ephraim, and Dan—
Lo, are not they all your brethren? They will
    help you—if they can."
Well he knew the tribes were trodden like the
    ripe grapes in the press;
Knew that there was fear and famine, bondage,
    weakness, and distress:
So he sat, as one that waiteth for a ripening fig
    to fall—
But he knew not of Jehovah, and he reckoned
    not with Saul.

Then the elders sent him tidings that they could
    no succor find:
On the morrow all the city would come forth for
    him to blind.
So King Nahash drank and feasted with the
    captains of his host,
While they praised the gods of Ammon: there
    was jest and mighty boast.
Then they lay them down to slumber, and the
    wine possessed them all—
For they knew not of Jehovah, and they reckoned
    not with Saul.

Saul came up with his battalion, while the mists
    of night lay wet;
In the thickets of the Yabis near the camp his
    ambush set.
Jonathan led up his slingers and his bowmen to
    the heights,
Whence, with stone and whistling arrow, they
    could vex the Ammonites.

JABESH GILEAD

Abner brought his ragged legion, armed with
    sickle, axe, and sword,
Lay in wait among the vineyards by the road
    to Jabbok Ford.
Still the camp lay wrapped in quiet: slumber
    deep was on them all;
For they knew not of Jehovah, and they reckoned
    not with Saul.

In the dawning of the morrow pealed a sudden
    trumpet-call,
Echoing from the hills like thunder—and the
    lightning-bolt was Saul.
From the gulley of the Yabis hornet-like the
    spearmen poured:
Saul struck down the drowsy watchers with his
    great two-handed sword.
And the slingstones and the arrows thick as rain
    came pelting down
From the archer-men and slingers on the hills
    above the town.
Half awake, the men of Ammon sallied from their
    tents to die—
For they recked not of Jehovah, and they wist not
    Saul was nigh.

Nahash came from his pavilion, with his ready bow
    in hand,
And his armor-bearer followed, with his buckler,
    spear, and brand.
And they stood a moment watching where the
    weapons rose and fell—
All the air was loud with tumult, shivering shield
    and battle-yell.
Saul was hewing in the vanguard, head and
    shoulders o'er his men,
And his cry, "The Lord is for us!" rose and fell, and
    rose again.

JABESH GILEAD

Nahash drew a feathered arrow from the quiver at his back,
And he said, "These dogs of Jacob have a lion in their pack."
Swift at Saul he sped the arrow, whistling o'er the stricken field:
Jethir leaped before his master, caught the shaft upon his shield.

Nahash marked the deed of valor: "May the gods of Ammon help!
Bare your teeth, ye wolves of Ammon, for the lion hath a whelp!"
Then he called his guard about him, set the lances in array,
Caught his brand and shield, and hastened to the thickest of the fray.
Now was Saul in bitter peril: death was crying in his ears,
For the ill-armed host of Israel flinched before the leveled spears.
Yet he held his ground, undaunted, Jethir laboring by his side,
And their swinging blades about them kept a circle deep and wide.
Then cried Nahash o'er the turmoil, "Mark yon chieftain of renown.
See ye save him from the slaughter. Death to him that strikes him down!"

Yet had Saul been surely taken, and an end of Israel's hope,
But that Jonathan found cattle feeding on a grassy slope.
There were Ammon's desert coursers; there were bullock, ox, and ass
Pillaged from the folk of Gilead, feeding on the upland grass.

JABESH GILEAD

And his men slung stones among them, till they
    moved and gathered speed,
Sweeping down the rocky hillside in a thunderous
    stampede;
And they rolled on Ammon's warriors, hemmed
    between the wall and wood,
With a thunder like the Jordan when its waters
    roll in flood;
And King Nahash saw his people trampled,
    scattered, overborne
By the fury of the onset, flying hoof and tossing
    horn.
And he leaped upon a courser, as it passed with
    flying mane,
Prodded on by bulls of Bashan, mad and screaming
    in its pain;
Caught and clung, escaped the ruin: but his soul
    within was gall,
That he had not feared Jehovah and he had not
    known of Saul.

Now the men of Israel, rallying, thrust with spear
    and hacked with sword,
Till all Ammon fled for Rabbah, by the road to
    Jabbok Ford.
Fled to die: for Abner's warriors from their ambush
    by the road
Hewed them down with axe and sickle, thrust them
    through with pike and goad;
And they lay, with scarlet gashes showing through
    their cloven mail,
Like the crimson ripe pomegranates split and
    scattered by the hail.
Yet a few escaped the slaughter, and to Rabbah
    carried back
Tidings that the dogs of Jacob had a lion in their
    pack.

JABESH GILEAD

Never more the hosts of Ammon came through
    Gad with sword and sling;
For they feared the Lord Jehovah, and they
    dreaded Saul the King.

The Philistines

I

From Crete they came of old,
The land of Minos and the Minotaur,
Fair-haired and tall, a people of the sea,
Who traced their lineage to that Titan race
That in the dawn of time, as legends told,
Had warred with gods. And mighty still in war
Where galleys churned the seas or chariots rolled,
Their power had shaken Pharaoh's mastery,
Wrenched Syria's sea-dunes from the Hittites' hold,
And dashed the gage of war in Sidon's face.

Their cities kept the roads
From Memphis to the gates of Babylon.
The heavy-footed caravans that came
From Nineveh, Carchemish, Hamath, Tyre,
And Ishmael's and Elam's far abodes,
Brought treasures of the merchant: there was none
But paid them tribute—dates and honey, loads
Of corn and almonds, gold like dusty flame,
Beasts of the desert cowering from the goads,
And captive maids, and gems of frozen fire.

The sea brought gifts of shell,
Lustrous and shimmering with the rainbow's hue,
Pearls, sandalwood, sweet incense, ivory, bales
Of blue and scarlet: for their galleys plied

THE PHILISTINES

The utmost ocean. Isles where ripples fell
Like sea-maid's kisses and the vales were blue
With hyacinth and iris, knew them well;
Far Ilium had seen their purple sails
Fade on Aegean's milk-and-azure swell,
And Nile had borne them on his sluggish tide.

Their tribes had each its lord,
The kings of Gaza, Ashkelon, and Gath,
Ashdod and Ekron. Arrogant and free,
Each lord in his dominions ruled alone.
But when, with javelin-stings, the desert horde
Buzzed round their walls like hornets, or the wrath
Of proud Phoenicia on their cities poured
Chariots by land and ships upon the sea,
Philistia girded on her flashing sword,
And all her cities faced the foe as one.

She saw her power increase
From little into much, from much to more:
Before her chariots fled the Amorite,
And Amalek retreated to the waste
Of sun and blinding sand. Her iron peace
Lay heavy on the coast: one foot on shore
And one upon the ocean, with its fleece
Of shaggy rollers thundering into white
Where rode her ships, she stood; nor would she cease
From conquests till the nations were abased.

All peoples feared her power:
Great Egypt, father of the nations, saw
Her armed heel treading on his waste frontiers,
And held his peace. Phoenicia strove in vain
Against her ships. Damascus in her flower,
And Midian who taught her desert law
To kingdoms, quailed to see the war-clouds lower,
Lit by the stormy lightning of her spears,
And feel her furious chariots shake the plain.

THE PHILISTINES

And then a people came,
In bondage long to Egypt, whom their God,
More strong than any that the nations knew,
Brought forth with wonders and a mighty hand,
And led them, in a shaft of cloud and flame,
Unscathed through deserts, over floods dry-shod,
And, making known through them His power and name,
He brought them over Jordan, to subdue
The Amorites, put Canaan's kings to shame,
And drive the Hivites from their mountain land.

Philistia then knew fears,
And she, who taught the mighty ones to quake,
Was filled with tremblings; for she heard the sound
Of combat and the shouts of victory
Draw nearer, till the tumult dinned her ears.
She felt her high-walled cities reel and shake
Before their onset; and her charioteers,
For all their fury, scarce could hold their ground,
Hemmed by the narrowing ring of Israel's spears,
Between the sand dunes and the climbing sea.

First Ekron fell a prey,
Then Gath: her outposts in the mountain land,
Where gullied hills gave shelter to the foe.
But in her triumph Israel found defeat;
Discovering here the images of clay
And stone and silver—all the horrid band
Philistia worshiped—and she turned away
From God to Baalzebub and Derketo,
Marna and fishy Dagon, and to lay
Her offerings before the gods of Crete.

And as on them who eat
The drowsy poppy or the lotus-leaf,
A dreamy and delicious languor steals
And numbs the senses, till the thews and bones
Are weak as cobwebs, and what seemed so sweet

THE PHILISTINES

Grows bitter unto death; and yet no grief
Nor penitence can free them, and they beat
The breast in anguish, and the reason reels,
And conscience falls from his imperial seat
To gibber like an ape among the stones;

Even thus o'er Israel drew
A dimness of the spirit. They were hard
Of limb, as in the days when victory's wings
Flashed o'er their host; but faintness, like a rust
That eats in secret, cankered brain and thew;
Sin sapped their souls. They wist not that the Lord
Was not among them, but Philistia knew:
Beneath the banners of her mighty kings
She burst upon them like a whirlwind, slew
Their mightiest men, and drave the rest as dust.

She set her iron yoke
Upon their shoulders, shackled foot and hand,
And made them pay her tribute from the fold,
The herd, the vineyard. Full four hundred years
They fawned like beaten dogs beneath her stroke;
Her mail-clad garrisons oppressed the land
From hilltop fortresses with gates of oak,
And through their vales her flashing chariots rolled
In pride of power; and from the wretched folk
She snatched the swords and took away the spears.

And though at times the land
Brought forth a champion, whom Jehovah's breath
Inspired with courage to resist the foe
And break the fetters that had held them thrall—
A Shamgar with an ox-goad in his hand,
A mad and hairy Samson, dealing death
With ass's bone, and toppling to the sand
Their crowded temple in one overthrow
Of gods and people—none for long could stand
Against their power, until the days of Saul.

THE PHILISTINES

II

O'er Israel, from Jordan to the sea,
Philistia's kings yet held their mastery:
Their runners came and went, their chariots whirled,
Unchallenged, where they would. Above the world,
Like eagles' nests, their citadels kept guard.
Their bondage weighed so heavy and so hard
That none had spirit left, except to lie
Before the altars of their gods, and cry
For succor, while they saw their corn and oil
Borne off, their sheep and cattle made a spoil;
And famine ever sat before the door,
And hope grew less, and fear grew more and more.

And thus the land was wasted and made bare.
The leopard and the lion made their lair
In villages where folk had dwelt of old;
Among the stones of ruined press and fold
The wild ass brayed; o'er crumbled altars, where
In olden days were offering and prayer,
The conies sported; bramble-bush and thorn
Grew thick in fields where once the yellowing corn
Had made the reapers glad with harvest feasts;
And men were few, and lived the lives of beasts.

But in Philistia there were sheep and kine
And figs and olives, and the russet vine
Where grapes grew purple in the Summer sun,
And feasting when the harvest days were done,
With harping in the streets, and laughing lips;
And far-off seas were splendid with her ships.

Yet Samuel, at Rama, where the Ark
Of God abode, still kept against the dark
A lamp of faith; and far in Benjamin,
By steep and rocky mountains circled in,
Had Saul laid up the battle-bow and sword
Against the day of vengeance of the Lord.

THE PHILISTINES

And word was brought to Achish, King of Gath,
How Saul had risen, mighty in his wrath,
Against King Nahash; how at his command
The tribes had gathered out of all the land
In one great host, and smitten Ammon's horde
From Jabesh Gilead unto Jabbok Ford.
Yea more: how after this the people drew
Together unto Gilgal, to renew
The kingdom there, and Samuel had poured
Libations at the altar of the Lord,
And Israel had sworn to put away
The Ashtaroth and Baalim, and obey
The Lord and Saul.

                Then Achish told these things
Before the council of Philistia's kings,
And said, "My Lords, ye know the man of old:
A robber and a rebel he, yet bold
And fierce and crafty; and his lawless hive
Of venomed mountain hornets yet contrive
To vex us with their stings. Howe'er we try
To smoke them out, they build their nest too high.
They gird our swords, and wear our coats of mail.
Lo then, if we in nothing might prevail
Against him when he ruled one feeble town,
How shall we prosper, now he wears the crown?"

Then answered Phicol, Ekron's lord, "Ye make
Great matter out of nothing. I will take
A thousand men, and chase him from the land;
Yea, with the butt of spear and flat of brand,
Will drive him like a hare."

                      "And wilt thou so?"
Said Achish. "By great Marna, we who know
The mettle of these men have found them like
Gazelles in speed, but lions when they strike."

THE PHILISTINES

>   Then answered Hanun, lord of Ashkelon,
>   "Who then shall give us counsel? There is none
>   Can tell us what in future shall betide,
>   Save those within whose spirits doth abide
>   The spirit of the gods. For these have power
>   To see far times as we the present hour.
>   Call in diviners: they shall tell us true
>   What Fate decrees, and counsel what to do."
>
>   And Achish said, "We have a captive maid
>   Whom Agag, Chief of Amalek, in a raid,
>   Took from the Hebrews: Pinaruta, priest
>   Of Dagon, bought her; and he hath not ceased
>   To teach her divination, so she hath
>   Excelled by far the oracles of Gath
>   In necromancy; for the august lord,
>   Our holy Dagon, speaketh in her word,
>   Revealing hidden things. Come, let us call
>   On her for counsel how to vanquish Saul."
>
>   So Pinaruta came, and with him brought
>   The captive maid, to whom he long had taught
>   His evil craft.
>   At first her spirit, clothed
>   In that pure faith by Samuel taught, had loathed
>   The priest and all his works; the rites obscene,
>   The amulets and potions, the unclean
>   And hellish charms. But when her master learned
>   That it was unto Saul her spirit turned
>   For help, as one to whom she must be true
>   As he to her, the priest around her threw
>   A trance enchanted, and by potent charms
>   He showed her lover sleeping in the arms
>   Of her deep-bosomed sister. Then she cried
>   A bitter, hopeless cry, and something died

THE PHILISTINES

Within her soul, and left her but a wraith
Of taunting memory. "There is no faith
In man or God. But teach me to forget,
And I will do thy will." The sorcerer set
His sign upon her, made her drink the cup
Brewed from the mandragora rooted up
In darkness, mingled with the pallid dew
Of Lethe's soundless waters; and she knew
The past no more.

              The devils, ere they fell
In sputtering lightnings to the gulf of Hell,
Were cherubim that walked the courts of God:
None fall so far as they who once have trod
The boundless splendor of celestial heights.
Henceforth she reveled in the horrid rites
That once she hated. Charms she learned, and spells
And incantations: from the deepest Hells
Would demons come, obedient to her word,
That worshiped Baalzebub as king and lord.
No longer was she fair, or starry-eyed;
But in her face were hopelessness and pride,
The fiends that slay the soul; and these had warred
On hers and withered it. Her trade abhorred
Had left her but the husk of womanhood,
Vile and despairing. Shameless now she stood
Unveiled before the kings.

                    Then Achish named
The name of Saul; and something in her flamed
That once was love. It flickered out and died,
Flickered again, and left her hollow-eyed
And trembling. She went groping through her mind
As men immured in dungeons grope, to find
A something lost: a bone, a mouldy crust
Of bread, among the rotting straw and dust,
But shuddering lest, amid the crumbled stones,
They touch a serpent or a dead man's bones,

THE PHILISTINES

A toad, a scorpion; and they half forget
What thing they sought, but go on groping yet—
So, through the murky blackness of her brain,
The dungeon of despair, where phantoms vain
Stirred in the dark, did Atarah's memory grope,
Unknowing what it sought, and void of hope.
And through her groping, like far cries of birds,
Sound without meaning, came to her the words
Of Achish: "Therefore now, O holy man,
Command, we pray, thine handmaid, that she scan
Futurity; that we, foreseeing what
The gods decree, Philistia perish not."

And faintly still, as through a dream, she heard
The lips of Pinaruta frame the word
Of incantation: such a potent spell
As opens Tartarus. The pit of Hell
Gaped wide before her; bottomless abyss
Of breathless blackness. She could hear the hiss
Of shadowy and innumerable wings
In that thin air; the crablike skitterings
Of formless horrors, moving in the slime
And stink of rottenness as old as time.
Then from the pit the darkness rose, and drew
Around her. Far away a trumpet blew,
And there were shoutings, and the fitful gleam
Of burning cities, seen as through a dream;
Even while her memory still groped, within
Its narrow prison, through despair and sin,
For something lost long since. Was it a name,
A prayer, a hope? Again the trumpet came:
The men of Israel were mustering fast;
And now Philistia's hosts went marching past,
Splendid in arms. She heard the shouts of men
That clash in arms; the trumpets blew again,
And chariots shook the earth. A wavering flood
Of war, with spray of steel and foam of blood,

THE PHILISTINES

Swayed doubtful to and fro; and in the van
Moved shadowlike a tall, dark-bearded man
That seemed a king.

                Now from Philistia's host
There came a champion forth, with haughty boast,
Defying Israel: a giant shape
In scaly mail, with shoulders like an ape,
His shield a moon, his spear a weaver's beam.
And now the Hebrew warrior that did seem
A king came out against him. She beheld
The giant's brawny arm, that might have felled
Behemoth, heaving up his sword to dash
The Hebrew headlong. Even in its flash
The fumbling fingers of her memory
Found what they sought: a whispering olive tree
In evening quietness; a stranger youth,
Whose eyes were honest as the eyes of Truth,
That sought for asses, and the olive's shade
Across his face. And still the giant's blade
Swung high in air. And from within her burst
A cry of anguish, and a name none durst
Utter in Gath—the name of Israel's Lord.
"Jehovah! God of Battles! Stay the sword!"
And with her crying out, a far-slung stone
Crashed on the giant, shattering casque and bone,
And laid him headlong. Then Philistia's pride
Like chaff before the wind was scattered wide,
While Israel triumphed. And she cried aloud,
"Jehovah! Thou hast overthrown the proud
And high of heart and the uncircumcised;
And them that were afflicted and despised
Hast lifted up, and set Thy people free,
Giving to Israel the victory!"

Unlawful words were these: the bearded kings
Muttered in wrath; the demons clapped their wings

THE PHILISTINES

    About her ears, and bared their filthy teeth
In impotence and wrath, while Hell beneath
Shook to its miry depths. Then from the height
Of Heaven an angel, like a bolt of light,
Descended with his lightning-scourge, and drave
The whimpering demons back into their cave
Of whispering darkness, and the brazen door
Clanged shut behind: the phantoms were no more.
But through her trance, with rude awakening, burst
The voice of Pinaruta: "Hag accursed!
The kings have summoned thee to prophesy
Against our foes. Then wherefore dost thou cry
On Israel's God?" And Hanun said, "Disown
The God of Israel. For thy sin atone,
On Saul denouncing death, defeat and shame."

    She answered, "By that Name I may not name,
Philistia's gods, by whom I prophesied,
I have abjured, and cast their power aside.
And by that Living One, whose word is breath
And spirit, though ye doom me to the death,
I have no power to curse where He hath blessed,
Nor bless where He hath cursed. At His behest
I tell thee that while Saul shall keep the law
Of Israel's God, your spears shall be as straw
Before him, and your chariots like to dust
Scattered and driven by the desert gust;
Your high-walled cities shall become as tow
Before the fire, and ye shall be brought low."

    Then Adimar of Ashdod gnawed his lips
In wrath, and cried to bring the scorpion-whips
And lash the witch to death. But Achish said,
"What profit will she bring us, being dead?
If she hath spoken truth, it will abide
The truth, though worms devour her. If she lied,

THE PHILISTINES

The time shall prove it. Scourge her hence, and bind
Her feet in iron fetters. Let her grind
The meal to make our bread. As oracle
She served us ill; yet she may serve us well
In other guise." Thereon the scourgers came,
With whips that cut like swords and burned like flame,
And lashed her to her prison; and the door
Rolled shut behind. A grayness stretched before
Of death in life—through all the days to be
To look no more on earth or sun or sea,
But toil in twilight, writhing with the pain
Of this her soul, long dead, that lived again.

But now the kings, perplexed and half dismayed
At these ill omens, where they looked for aid
Of ghostly counsels, sat debating long
What might amend their case, what make them strong
Against King Saul. And still did Phicol urge
That he would go, with but a staff and scourge,
And drive the loutish fellow from his hills.
His loud insistence bent at last their wills
To his design. By holy Derketo
And Marna, let him take his scourge, and go!
But Dagon help him if he came to grips
With Saul! And, by his leave, they would send ships,
Urged both by sail and oar, across the foam
To Sicily, and bring Goliath home.
Their giant champion, master of the seas
From Asia to the Gates of Hercules,
The scourge of Sidon, treader-down of ships,
Whose warlike fame had never known eclipse.
A thrust of spear, a single stroke of brand,
From him, should vanquish Saul, and leave his land
Defenseless: there was neither god nor man
Had stood against him, since his wars began.

THE PHILISTINES

    No counsel this of Achish: for the King
Of Gath had scanty cause for welcoming
The giant home. Although his subject, born
In his dominions, he had known his scorn
And rivalry of old, and there was reason
To look for turbulence and open treason
If he returned to Gath. But still the rest
Cried down his doubts, insisting this were best
For all Philistia. True it was, when young,
The man had wagged a wild and rebel tongue
Against his sovereign; but his years of war
With Tyre and Sidon and the King of Dor,
The treasures he had gathered from the nests
Of all the earth, his ships that churned the crests
Of utmost ocean, and his hundred sails
That dipped the brine and thundered in the gales
And cowed the nations to the wide world's edge—
These things had taught him wisdom: they
      would pledge
Their kingly faith to Achish, and would stand
His sureties, that the man should lift no hand
Against his peace. And Achish, though he saw
His peril, yielded to Philistia's law
And to the council's will, and seemed compliant
With what they purposed. Yet he knew the giant
A rebel to his laws, a rival bold
And void of mercy.

               For in days of old,
When Samson came from Judah for a wife,
Ere she beguiled him and betrayed his life,
His iron strength, commingling with the grim
Old Titan blood, begat the Anakim,
Like those of old the spies of Moses found
In Kiriath Arba and the region round,
Before whose monstrous stature common men
Were but as locusts. Ever and again

At Gaza or at Gath there would arise
One of that race, of such gigantic size
As theirs who warred with Jove. And such an one
Goliath was. Beneath the wheeling sun
Was not a man, though girt with mail, might stand
One buffet from the champion's open hand.
And he it was the council planned to bring
And match in single fight with Saul the King.

III

King Saul had picked three thousand men,
Of those who crossed the ford again
   With dinted blades and shields
From Jabesh; and the rest he sent
To ploughman's hut and shepherd's tent
   To tend their flocks and fields.
But these were tried in warfare grim
And proved. Two thousand were with him
   Encamped on Michmash height;
At Gibeah a second band
Obeyed Prince Jonathan's command,
   And kept their weapons bright.

Yet, though the rout of Ammon's chief
Had overawed the desert thief,
   And raiders came no more,
Philistia still oppressed the folk
With sack and outrage, and her yoke
   Was heavier than before.
And Jonathan beheld the land
Devoured and plundered, and his hand
   Burned to avenge the wrong
On Geba; but its gates were barred
With bronze; its walls were high and hard:
   The citadel was strong.
And, having neither ram nor tower,

THE PHILISTINES

He ground his teeth and bode his hour.
  But now and then his wrath
Surprised the plunderers as they sacked,
And from their hands the fingers hacked,
  And sent them back to Gath.

Then marched King Phicol with his band,
To drive the rebels from the land
  And burn their hiding-place:
A thousand men he had, the flower
And splendor of the martial power
  Of Ekron's warlike race.
Earth shook beneath their haughty tread,
Their lances flashed; and overhead
  King Phicol's standard flew,
And, moving with its rippling fold,
There rolled two dolphins, wrought in gold,
  Upon a sea of blue.

Now Phicol's warriors held but scorn
For Saul; a yokel, meanly born,
  That called himself a king:
Before them went no watchful spies;
No pickets guarded from surprise
  Assault on van or wing.
Half-armed they marched, with bucklers slung
On back, and helms at girdle hung:
  Relaxed was every rule,
And men would straggle off to loot
A wine-press or a grove of fruit,
  Like boys escaped from school,
While king and captains set at naught
The power of Saul. And runners brought
  The word to Jonathan,
Who with his band at Gibeah lay,
How Phicol's men made holiday
With song and jest, along the way
  That runs by Aijalon.

THE PHILISTINES

And Jonathan, to whom the ways
By wild ass trod and goats at graze,
   Were known for miles around,
Arose, and moved his band by night
By rough ravine and craggy height,
And stream-beds where the sand lay white,
   And over thorny ground;
At morning, when the thickets stood
Enwreathed with mist, they reached the wood
   Before Beth-aven. There
The road ran past to Geba's gate,
And here he gave command to wait
   And ambuscade prepare.

The wait was short: before the sun
Had dried the mist, from Aijalon
   Was heard the war-drum's beat,
The clank of harness, and the sound
Of marching men: the sullen ground
   Shook with the tramp of feet.
The spears flashed back the sunlight fair,
The golden dolphins swam in air
Above their heads; and unaware
King Phicol marched into the snare:
   It was a gallant thing
To see Philistia's warriors come,
With flash of armor, roll of drum,
   And scornful trumpeting.

In woodland shade each Israelite
Set shaft upon his string aright,
   A second stuck in earth
Beside him, ready to his hand,
And waited, while Philistia's band
   Came on with heedless mirth.
Then, like a harp, the Prince's string
Twanged sharp and clear: the foolish King

　　　　Fell, cloven through the brain.
　　And now, transfixing breast and head,
　　From bush and tree the arrows sped
　　　　Like pattering drops of rain.
　　Full half the band lay choked in blood;
　　And ere the others, as they stood
　　Surprised and crowded in the wood,
　　　　Could get their swords unsheathed,
　　The Hebrews from their ambush broke
　　And hewed them down with thrust and stroke,
　　　　Till there was none that breathed.

　　Then Jonathan's companions stripped
　　Their foemen's armor, and equipped
　　　　Their limbs with coats of mail;
　　They bound the cuirass on the breast,
　　Put on the helm, with plumy crest;
　　　　Nor did their prudence fail
　　To gird Philistia's glittering blade
　　And brace the buckler. Thus arrayed,
　　　　With flash of steel and gold,
　　While Phicol's trumpets shrilly blew
　　And Phicol's standard o'er them flew,
　　　　They moved on Geba's hold.

IV

On Geba's ramparts, when the day was done,
Broke the last arrows of the setting sun,
And all to westward, though the skies were proud
With ruddy light, where flecks of golden cloud
Like burning galleys flamed, the vales were blue
With deepening shadows, and the twilight drew
Her mantle o'er the hills; the road was dim
With dusk, and vanished ere it reached the rim
Of the horizon. It was nigh the hour
To change the watch: the warder in his tower

THE PHILISTINES

Above the gateway stretched his muscles, numb
With weight of armor, hearkening for the drum
To beat before the guard-room, and he heard
Instead a call of trumpets: something stirred
Along the winding way to Aijalon,
Now seen, now lost: against the sinking sun
Flashed lance and harness, and a rippling fold
Of standard, with device of blue and gold,
Moved in the wind. That banner well he knew:
He roused his comrades with a glad halloo
That men came marching up the hill, arrayed
In helm and mail, and over them displayed
King Phicol's golden dolphins waved in pride
Upon their sea of blue. The gate swung wide
In welcome, and the garrison poured out
To greet their countrymen with merry shout.

But while the moving column in its march
Was yet a stone's-cast from the granite arch,
Came forth the captain, and his fury burst
Upon the warder's head. "Thou fool, accursed
Of all the gods! Thou harlot's whelp! Shut fast
The gate, or else this folly is thy last!
Ye witless yokels, get within the wall
And gird your weapons. Let the trumpet call!"

The warder, in his tower above the gate,
Sprang to obey—but sprang a breath too late.
Before his fingers closed upon the bar
A feathered shaft came flying fast and far
From Israel's ranks: for Shammah, Jethir's son,
Who bare in war the shield of Jonathan,
Had drawn a bow of might. The arrow passed
Through bronze and bone, and pinned the watchman fast,
To writhe, transfixed, against the oaken beam
In mortal agony. His horrid scream
Was blent with Israel's exultant shout
As swift they charged the gate with weapons out.

THE PHILISTINES

    Yet in his death the warder nigh undid
The folly of his life. His fingers slid
Along the beam, and grasped the bar that swung
The gate, and with his final breath he sprung
The catch, and died. But as the gate began
To turn on groaning hinges, Jonathan
Had gained the entrance: at a single thrust
Of Phicol's blade the captain rolled in dust
Gnawing his tongue in torment, and the door
Crushed out his brains, and jammed, and moved no more.

    And now about the portal furious strife
Began: the aliens, battling for their life,
Half-armed, uncaptained, taken unaware,
Fought with the reckless valor of despair.
They flung themselves upon the swords that hewed
Among them, and with unrelenting feud
They strove to bear their foemen to the field,
Or drive the dagger-point through mail and shield.
But Israel fought in vengeance of the long
Oppression of four hundred years of wrong.
She fought for home and kindred; for the land
Sworn to her fathers, with uplifted hand,
By God of old. Endued with helm and shield,
She now must triumph, or forever yield.
She fought in hope. At length the press of swords
Carried the gate, and then the inner wards:
Through streets and open ways the battle spread,
The air was thick with shouts, and earth was red,
And overhead the sky grew black with night,
While still, from wall to citadel, the fight
Raged on. The few defenders, hard beset
From every quarter, but unyielding yet,
Died as the cattle in the shambles die,
In huddled heaps, with the exultant cry
Of Israel in their ears.

THE PHILISTINES

               The sword had wrought
Its bitter vengeance. Now the torch was brought,
With branches from the wood and heaps of straw,
And snapping teeth of flame began to gnaw
At tower and barracks, where those few, whom fear
Had driven from the battle, fled the spear
And sword, to meet a yet more dreadful doom:
With burning hair they rushed from room to room,
And died like vermin, while the wings of fire
Soared over them in one vast funeral pyre
That dimmed the stars.

                       The watchmen on far peaks
Beheld the beacon flame, and to their cheeks
The hot blood surged, with that high ecstasy
None know, except the vanquished when they see
The conqueror conquered. Then the tide withdrew
And left them cold and pale: for well they knew
The torch that flamed at Geba was a brand
To kindle fiery vengeance on their land—
A vengeance that would trample and consume
Till Israel triumphed, or went down to doom.

And Saul beheld, and sounded far and near
The trumpet, saying, "Let the Hebrews hear!"

Michmash

I

When the dread news to Ekron came
Of Geba given to sword and flame,
And Phicol's lusty band waylaid
And slaughtered in Beth-aven's shade,
   Fierce was the tumult then:
The air was loud with milling feet
And women wailing in the street
   And shouts of angry men.

When kings and lords in council met,
The cheeks of some with tears were wet,
   And some with wrath were pale.
Mitinti, son of Ekron's lord,
Came armed with dagger and with sword,
   And girt in coat of mail
That shook with sobs of grief and rage,
While like a lion in his cage
   He paced the council hall;
And oft his blade he half unsheathed,
While furious threatenings he breathed
   On Jonathan and Saul.

And though King Achish counseled well
That chiefs like Saul were hard to quell,
And that they best had count the cost
In blood poured out and treasure lost

MICHMASH

Ere banners on the wind were tossed,
   The others cried him down,
And vowed that naught but blood and steel
And captives dragged at chariot-wheel
Philistia's prowess could reveal
   And cleanse her fair renown.
Then young Mitinti sware an oath
By Baalzebub and Dagon both
   That to avenge his sire,
From Carmel's crest to Jordan's ford
He'd harrow Israel with his sword
   And harvest it with fire.

So all the Council cried for war:
And straight, from Gaza unto Dor,
   Were mustered for the fray
The chariot with its rumbling wheel,
The spearmen, groves of flashing steel,
   The horsemen in array,
And numberless as ocean sands
The pikes and javelins and brands,
   The archers and the slings;
With roll of drums and trumpet's blare,
While o'er them rippled, broad and fair,
   The banners of the kings.
So were it if a thousand men
Should track a weasel to his den
   With lances laid in rest,
Or hosts of Nineveh and Tyre
Should march in mail, with sword and fire,
   To sack a hornet's nest.

Then, lest this power should be too small
To match against the might of Saul,
They called the desert thieves; each clan
Of Ishmael and Midian,
   By Abraham begot,

MICHMASH

The faithless sons of faithful man,
 And Moab, son of Lot,
And Amalek, the thorny weed
 That sprang from Esau's lawless seed,
And said to them, "Make haste:
The field we fenced for wine and corn
Brings forth but bramble-bush and thorn:
 Come up and lay it waste.
No longer dwell with burning sand:
Behold, we give you all the land
 Where Israel hath been—
A land of olive, fig and vine,
With pasturage for sheep and kine:
Drive out these stinking Hebrew swine,
 And ye shall dwell therein."

So from the West, with mighty force,
Philistia's armies, foot and horse
 And furious chariots, pour,
With pikes and standards waving wide,
Like some resistless ocean-tide,
 Tumultuous in its roar;
And from the desert's burning sand,
Darkening the earth like locust band,
The Bedouins devastate the land
 And sweep it bare before.

II

Then, as he could, the King had gathered head
 At Gilgal to withstand them. But how few,
How piteously armed, how faint with dread,
 Were they that thither drew

To tremble after him in sore dismay,
 While every post brought tidings that the foe
Moved on to crush them! Every passing day
 Saul watched their terror grow.

But Samuel the Seer had sent him word
    To tarry yet at Gilgal seven days,
Till he should come, and offer to the Lord
    The gifts of peace and praise.

"And see," he said, "thou keep the Lord's command,
    Although thy power like snow shall melt away;
For God will give the battle to thine hand.
    Be faithful, and obey."

And Saul had waited, even while his mind
    Grew bitter unto death, as hour by hour
He heard the trumpets screaming down the wind,
    And watched his dwindling power.

For there was such a terror on his men
    As shakes a flock of sheep with tremblings dumb,
That hear the wolf-pack howling in the glen
    Or see the lion come.

And day by day they faded from his sight
    And hid in pits or caves; or, driven half mad
With fear, across the Jordan took their flight
    To Reuben and to Gad;

While Abner ever urged him on to strike
    One blow at least, stake all upon the chance
Of battle, while he yet had shield or pike
    To stem the foe's advance,

Or, if he durst not venture stroke so bold,
    At least to leave this undefended plain
And lie at Gibeah, his trusty hold
    In many a past campaign.

And though he sent to Samuel, to urge
    That he would come and aid him in his plight,
Since all his company were on the verge
    Of mutiny and flight,

MICHMASH

The Prophet answered only with the words,
  "Abide at Gilgal till I come to thee.
The battle and the power are the Lord's:
  He giveth victory."

So, wavering between despair and hope,
  Saul tarried yet. The Philistines came nigher,
Wasting the country, village, vale and slope,
  With all-devouring fire;

While, terrible as Hell, the desert host
  Came swarming o'er the mountains from the South;
And Gilgal camp was like a lamb, almost
  Within the lion's mouth.

The seventh day dawned: morn passed, and burning noon,
  And brought no sign or message from the Seer.
The long day waned. Oh, if he came not soon—
  Saul's heart was sick with fear.

For scarce a thousand warriors yet abode,
  With Saul, who eyed him with a baleful glare
Like fierce and maddened beasts; and Abner chode
  Till he was in despair:

"Art thou the King?" he said, "and dost thou wait
  For this wild Prophet till thy realm is wrecked?
I tell thee, Saul, the case is desperate:
  Nor needest thou expect

"That I will tarry longer. By the hilt
  Of this good blade, if thou wilt strike one blow
For Israel's cause, I follow where thou wilt.
  If not, then I will go

"And seek for safety in the Land of Gad;
  And these will follow, be assured of that.
Then see if thou, and this old man gone mad,
  Can lay Philistia flat."

MICHMASH

Between his growing wrath at Samuel,
   And fear, Saul's wavering resolution broke:
"I thank thee, Abner; thou hast spoken well,
   And I will strike the stroke.

"For am I not anointed of the Lord
   The King of Israel, to lead, command—
Or but a dog, to answer Samuel's word,
   And fawn, and lick his hand?

"Behold, it is the hour of offering:
   The shadows grow; the sun descends the skies.
And I will be, to-day, both priest and king,
   And burn the sacrifice."

So, all in haste, before his fury cool,
   Half fearful lest the trembling in his bones
Should stay his hand and make him seem a fool,
   He heaped the altar-stones

And laid the wood in order; bade his men
   Lead forth a bullock for the sacrifice—
And then his purpose faltered once again:
   He stood with downcast eyes,

And first he felt his blood run fiery hot,
   Then cold as ice, as with an ague's siege.
A voice within him whispered, "Do it not!
   This deed were sacrilege."

Oh, what a field of conflict is the soul!
   What swords are there unsheathed, what lances thrust,
What shields are rent, what furious chariots roll,
   What champions writhe in dust!

But when the field is held by Wrath and Pride,
   Let Faith be strong, and armed in triple mail!
And if the lance of Fear shall prick his side,
   Seldom shall Faith prevail.

MICHMASH

    The King was vanquished ere the strife began:
        Pride, Wrath, and Fear, fell champions of the gloom,
    Assailed at once the spirit of the man
        And bore him down to doom.

    In fear he struck: he felt the hot blood spurt
        Against his cheek, and heard the people shout.
    The dying bullock wallowed in the dirt:
        And now he felt no doubt

    That he had acted well. For oft defeat
        Goes trapped like triumph, and her hand bestows
    A peace and exaltation all as sweet
        As hard-won victory knows.

    And now he knelt, with light upon his face
        And hope in heart, assured his deed was good;
    Cut up the offering, laid each piece in place,
        And fired the wood.

    The men stood bowed of head and worshiping;
        The roasting collops sizzled in the fire,
    Which lit, with rosy flickerings, host and King:
        The pale blue smoke rose higher.

    The deed was done: the fire had sunk to red
        And silvery coals, almost devoid of flame.
    Across the camp the lengthening shadows spread:
        And then the Prophet came.

    He marked the altar, and the smoke ascending
        In windless air against the setting sun,
    And in his face were pain and grief unending.
        He asked, "What hast thou done?"

    The King replied, "The folk were scattered from me,
        And thou thyself hadst tarried overlong.
    I feared the Philistines would overcome me:
        Thou seest, we are not strong.

"And if I waited, we should be defeated,
    For all men feared. I durst not draw the sword
For Israel, until I had entreated
    The favor of the Lord.

"The seven days were past; and I had waited
    For thee to come, far longer than was wise.
I forced myself, seeing thou wast belated,
    And offered sacrifice."

The Prophet said no word till Saul had spoken,
    But stood in silence, weighing every word,
Though in his heart he knew the King had broken
    The purpose of the Lord.

"And well for thee, instead of offering cattle,
    If thou hadst tarried yet another hour
For Him who leads the chariot forth to battle,
    The army and the power.

"God hath no pleasure in the offerings made Him
    By disobedient and rebellious hands:
But He had honored thee, hadst thou obeyed Him
    And honored His commands.

"Hast thou not heard of Shamgar and of Gideon
    (Thou who wast hopeless that so few abode)
Who brake Philistia and the yoke of Midian
    With naught but lamp and goad?

"His arm is strong, to save by few or many,
    By torch and tent-pin as by bow and sword.
Yet gives He not the victory unto any
    That trust not in His word.

"The Lord will not accept this offering brought him,
    Seeing thee hard and unbelieving still.
Thy kingdom shall not stand: for He hath sought Him
    A King to do His will."

MICHMASH

So Samuel spake, and gat him from the place.
   The moonless dark came up and covered all;
But there was deeper darkness on the face
   And in the heart of Saul.

He lay upon the earth; and though he heard
   Faint rustlings as the people stole away,
He sought not to detain them, said no word:
   What word was left to say?

At last he rose: the darkness robed the world;
   There was no light nor motion in the camp.
Into such night he saw his kingdom hurled—
   Dark, without sound or lamp.

And then he marked a figure lingering near,
   Pale as the fire-ash, silent as a ghost—
His uncle, Abner, leaning on his spear,
   The Captain of his host.

He said, "O Abner, thou and I have spent
   A life of toil, sword-stroke and javelin-thrust,
To build this realm, which now our hands have rent
   And tumbled down to dust,

"In one hour's madness. Why dost thou not go,
   Since all the rest forsake their King and flee?
God yet may save His people from the foe,
   But not by me."

And Abner said, "I brought thee to this plight.
   If sin it were (which yet I own not now:
It seemed most wise), then I must bear the blight
   No less than thou.

"If God forsake us, we have still our hands,
   And wills inured to peril and unease.
There have been kingdoms built from desert sands
   With less than these.

"Yea, more: we have our weapons; and we know
   The mountain pathways as a fox his hole.
Take courage; for we yet may strike a blow
   To vex Philistia's soul.

"Come then, my lord, and let us make our way
   To Gibeah, where the noble Jonathan
(Unless the hold were taken yesterday)
   Yet keeps his garrison.

"He hath six hundred—men that did not cringe
   From Phicol's warlike legion in the wood,
Who wrenched the gates of Geba from their hinge,
   And drenched the place with blood."

And so the twain—the King without a crown,
   The chief without an army—made their way
Through hills beset with foes, and reached the town
   About the dawn of day.

And there the King abode in fear, nor drew
   His sword, nor dared to risk encounter grim
Against the Philistines, since well he knew
   God had forsaken him.

Day after day he watched the invading force
   Flay bare the country to the rugged stone;
And like a maggot in his heart, remorse
   Gnawed till it made him groan.

III

It was the end of Summer, and the sun
   Blazed down upon a land as iron hard,
And dead with drouth. Fair blossom there was none;
   The grass was withered from the scanty sward.
Summer was dead, nor Autumn yet begun:
   The brooks were dry, and all the thickets marred.

MICHMASH

The cloudless heaven was a shield of steel,
   The earth beneath was dressed in drab attire;
The dust lay dry as ashes under heel,
   And hushed for heat was all the insect choir
Save one cicada, with his droning wheel,
   That ground the stillness into flakes of fire.

Prince Jonathan had stolen forth to view
   The desolation where the spoilers went;
The smoke-clouds dark against the windless blue,
   And field and village in wild ruin blent:
If there were but some deed that he could do,
   How gladly would he hazard the event!

Inaction galled him till he well could weep,
   Yet fell to gloomy reverie instead,
Too sad for tears. Below, the thorny steep
   Of Seneh dropped into the torrent's bed,
And o'er against it, like a giant's keep,
   The Crag of Bozez raised its shining head.

Its buttressed top was like an island set
   In seas of shimmering sunlight, with a wreath
Of smoke from morning camp-fires lingering yet
   In listless air above; and far beneath,
'Mid splintered stones, the shrunken rivulet
   Writhed like a serpent in a dragon's teeth.

Beyond the gorge, Philistia held the Range
   Of Michmash: he could see the glint of tents
And chariots, and might have watched them change
   The guard; but trusting to the battlements
Of rock, they kept no watch. Nor was it strange:
   The ridge was safe enough from all offense.

And yet, if one or two could scale the height,
   Endowed with courage and a dauntless will,

MICHMASH

Assail the garrison by shadowy light
  Of dusk or daybreak, and begin to kill—
A dubious venture this, but one that might
  In panic terror drive them from the hill.

Then, on his sorrowing meditation stole
  His armor-bearer, bringing him his sword
And harness. "Prince, my soul is as thy soul:
  In blood and sinew I am thine, my lord.
Our wound is deep; if thou canst make it whole,
  Reveal thy will, and I obey thy word."

And Jonathan made answer, "O my friend,
  Mine eyes have wept till they are dry as dust
And have no tears. But rather than to spend
  Our lives like hunted foxes, while the rust
Of fear eats out our vitals, let us end
  This profitless existence in one thrust

"Against the oppressor. Was it all in vain
  We brake the host of Phicol, and the door
Of Geba—to be trodden down like grain
  And blown as chaff upon the threshing-floor,
While still we watch my father's kingdom wane,
  Philistia's iron might wax more and more?

"There is a way by which a man may climb
  On hand and foot yon cliff of towering stone,
By dripping waters worn in olden time—
  A way the clambering ibex hath not known:
But clinging to the cracked and treacherous lime
  Will tax the breath, and well may break the bone.

"Shall we essay it? There the pagans keep
  But one or two to watch, or none at all,
And trust their safety wholly to this deep
  And savage gorge, and to the towering wall
Of precipice, so perilous and steep
  They deem that none can climb it. If we fall,

MICHMASH

"The end is only death: a wrench of pain
    That we have chanced full often. If thou wilt,
We hazard the adventure. If we gain
    The summit, heathen blood shall there be spilt
Before they hew us down; and I am fain
    To die in combat, with my hand on hilt."

Then Shammah answered, "Dost thou know the word
    Unto thy father spoken by the Seer
At Gilgal, that, though mighty nations gird
    The blade and buckler, and the charioteer
Lash on his steeds to fury, yet the Lord
    Shall break the bow of battle and the spear?

"I well believe that God hath moved thine heart
    To this adventure; and whate'er may skill
Of life or death, I would be as thou art,
    Of dauntless valor. Hasten to fulfill
Thy purpose, then; and if we do our part,
    The Lord shall give the victory if He will."

And Jonathan replied, "O loyal friend
    And hardy soldier, whom I ever prized,
As good in counsel as where weapons rend
    The helm and shield! Thy words are well advised.
We put them to the proof: we will descend
    And show ourselves to these uncircumcised.

"If they shall bid us stand, by this we know
    God goes not with us. But if their command
Shall be, 'Come up to us, and we will show
    A thing to you,' we then shall understand
The Lord hath sent us, and undoubting go,
    And He shall give the battle to our hand."

So down they clambered. Thorny thickets lent
    But scant and treacherous hold; and oft they took

MICHMASH

A perilous slide: their flesh was torn and rent
  By thorn and jagged stone and bramble-hook;
But at the last, all breathless and forspent,
  Yet safe, they stood beside the shrunken brook,

A trickle, hardly more, half hid by vines
  And boulders, though when swelled by wintry rain
It rolled a torrent. Here they plucked the spines
  From feet and hands, and washed away the stain
Of dust and clotted blood. The Philistines
  Looked down, and flung them mockery and disdain:

"Behold, the Hebrews issue from their caves
  To give us battle. Mark their strong array,
And tremble at the flash of spears and glaives!
  What bows and shields they muster for the fray!
Come up! Is not the Lord a God who saves?
  Hath He not given you victory this day?"

"Hear how these godless heathen," Shammah said,
  "Blaspheme the God of Israel; how they mock
Our feeble power, heap scorn upon our head,
  And hold us in derision. May the shock
Of tempest and of earthquake strike them dead;
  God's lightnings hurl them headlong from the rock!"

"Yea," said the Prince, "for they have prophesied!
  God's oracle is in their taunting tones.
Though they exalt themselves to heaven in pride,
  They shall be humbled to the dusty stones.
To-morrow shall their power be scattered wide,
  The raven and the fox shall pick their bones!

"Come then: there linger yet some hours of day.
  When God gives work to do, He gives the time.
We hazard Israel's hopes on this assay,
  And trust in God." And with a faith sublime,
Though hope seemed none, the warriors picked their way
  Across the brook, and soon began to climb.

MICHMASH

But Saul abode in Gibeah with his men—
    The same that at Beth-aven had withstood
King Phicol, and at Geba once again
    Had stormed the gate—now void of hardihood,
Like hunted vermin cowering in their den
    That hear the dogs run howling through the wood.

As far as eye could see, the land was given
    To fire and desolation: all the roads
Were thronged with spoiling bands, and captives driven
    Like herds of huddled beasts before the goads,
While men cried out against unpitying Heaven,
    And women wailed about their burned abodes.

And Saul himself was all but in despair,
    Well knowing it was for his sin the Lord
Was not with Israel, and had left him bare
    Of power to stand against the invading horde.
A smell of burning filled the breathless air,
    And high in heaven the kite and raven soared.

And such a little sin it was, he thought,
    And prompted by such hard necessity
Of utmost danger. He had only sought
    To make the people of Jehovah free—
Not in rebellion or presumption wrought;
    And Samuel quite as much to blame as he.

Yea, more to blame! For if the Seer had come
    One hour before, he had not done the deed.
And this, of his offending, was the sum:
    To seek the Lord in hour of utmost need.
He watched the ruin round him, and was dumb:
    What use to cry? Jehovah would not heed.

And there was Abner, who had pricked him on
    To that accursed folly, and the host

Cowering like curs, half slunk away and gone,
   While terror stalked through Gilgal like a ghost;
His army less with each succeeding dawn,
   And Samuel's tarrying— Yea, he blamed him most!

And was it just for God to take away
   The kingdom He had promised when the oil
Was poured upon his head by Samuel; yea,
   And all that he, through thankless years of toil
Had hardly won—un-king him in a day,
   And give the house of Israel to the spoil?

And such a little sin! Oh, wrong no doubt,
   But he had done it half against his will:
Nigh mad he was, and buffeted about
   By dreadful fears; and Abner teasing still—
He heard afar the foe's exulting shout,
   Their scornful trumpets sound from Michmash Hill.

A life of toil: and this was his reward!
   Entreaty and remorse alike were vain.
He cursed himself, and girded at the Lord
   In wordless wrath, and gnawed his tongue for pain,
His strong hands gripped upon his useless sword,
   And watched the smoke-wreaths drift along the plain.

IV

Saul groaned. But Jonathan and Shammah clomb
The Cliff of Bozez. All the fiery dome
Of heaven was an oven, and the stone
A blistering brand that burnt them to the bone.
No shade was there; not even a blasted thorn
Could find a foothold on that crag forlorn;
But here and there a nettle's withered stalk
Sprang from a fissure in the leprous chalk
And stung them with its spines. Dead dearth and heat
Were all around them, and beneath their feet

MICHMASH

The crumbling stone; and farther yet beneath
The splintered rocks like grinning dragon-teeth
That snarled with malice; while above them high
The bare white crag assailed the bare blue sky.

By hand and foot they clomb: an inch, an ell,
Through smothering heat, as if they crawled through Hell.
And then to heat and toil came parching thirst,
Withering their vitals, till they could have cursed
The hour they ventured on a task so mad.
Yet still they clomb: no other thought they had
Than reach the crest, though what they sought for there
They half forgot, and did not greatly care.

On yet. An inch, a span, a foot, a yard:
Their blood was boiling, and their breath came hard
In shuddering gasps. The pulse was like a drum,
The flesh worn raw and bleeding, fingers numb
With clinging to the fissures; palsied knees
Trembled beneath them. Once a swarm of bees
Poured from a cleft, to vex with fiery stings.
A viper hissed. And then a bat's dark wings
Brushed them in passing—for the afternoon
Was ended, and the brightening crescent moon
Beheld them climbing still.
                             The darkness drew
Around them, misty gray and dusky blue.
The crag above still held a shadowy light
A little while, and then the deep of night
Engulfed the world. The moon sloped down the sky
Beyond far hills. They did not know how high
They now had come, nor what remained to climb;
But still they clambered on, while Life and Time
Stood still to watch. Like spiders on a wall
They hung 'twixt earth and sky.

MICHMASH

                       The son of Saul,
Who led the way, had paused for breath, and heard,
Hoarse as the croak of some disgusting bird
The voice of Shammah speaking: "Jonathan,
The Lord be with thee... but my strength is done."
He ended on a gasp. But now the Prince
Had caught another sound: one heard long since
Before he passed through Hell; the tinkling drip
Of water, trickling from a mossy lip
Of stone, to drop into a fern-girt pool...
There must be rushes round it, and the cool
Of fragrant grasses. Did his senses mock,
Or had the Lord brought water from the rock
As once at Meribah? Again he strained
His ears to hearken: still the sound remained—
A soft and silvery murmur. Never pipe
Nor harp, when virgins danced and grapes were ripe,
Made sound so sweet! He moved his lips to speak:
His tongue was dry as ashes, and his cheek
Parched like a potsherd. With a gasping breath,
Faint as the rumble in the throat of death,
He whispered, "Shammah! as the Heaven is high,
Jehovah hath not brought us here to die.
A spring is near—almost within a span."
No answer came, but Jonathan began
To climb once more, and he could hear the beat
Of Shammah's heart almost beneath his feet,
And knew he followed. For another rood
They clambered, breathless but with hope renewed,
And then the Prince reached up to feel the bare
Face of the rock, and touched but vacant air.

Fumbling, he found some hold, and drew himself
Trembling and faint, upon a narrow shelf,
And Shammah followed. They were on a ledge
Nigh to the crest, as if a Titan's wedge

MICHMASH

    Had split the crag. A fig had taken root
Against the rock: they smelled the pungent fruit
And heard the foliage rustling in the wind.
And half beneath the tree and half behind,
Shimmering like velvet in the starlight dim,
A rock-rimmed basin rippled to the brim
With living water. Down on knee they sank,
And drank, and paused to breathe again, and drank,
And laughed for joy, and plunged their blistered scars
Deep in the pool among the leaves and stars,
With thanks to God unvoiced, and drank again,
And felt the water's coolness ease their pain
Like healing balm. And listening they heard,
Like drowsy twitterings of a dreaming bird
That sings in sleep, or laughter of brown elves,
The gurgling water tumbling over shelves
Of rock, in caverns hidden underground—
Some fissure of the cliff. The gentle sound
Went on and on, and blent with reveries
Half thought, half dreamed: the hum of hiving bees,
The breath of winds among the pasture grass,
The tinkle of the bells where camels pass,
Flutes, zithers, timbrels—all the sounds that sweep
Like little winds around the doors of sleep,
And lull the brain to rest, until their stiff
And aching limbs they stretched upon the cliff
And slept like babes.

                The stars, with measured march,
In bright battalions trode the soundless arch
Above them, and the world spun slowly on
To meet the fair fulfillment of the dawn,
While still they dreamed. But in the misty gray
That comes between the dawning and the day,
The ears of Jonathan, by peril taught
To listen through his deepest slumbers, caught

MICHMASH

A warning sound: a stone dislodged, or feet
That moved upon the ledge; and not the beat
Of Rusa's drums, nor Hanun's trumpet-blast,
Had quicklier roused him. Like a robe he cast
His sleep aside, leapt up, and stood at guard,
One foot advanced, the other planted hard
To meet what shock might come, his blade unsheathed,
And looked about.
               As yet the crag was wreathed
With vapory garlands, and the gorge below
Lay lapped in shadows; but a lurid glow
Suffused the east, the harbinger of storm.
Beside the spring there moved a shadowy form
Among the shadows; he could half discern
The hooded mantle, and the earthen urn
On shoulder borne, the slope of hip and breast—
A woman of the Philistines, he guessed,
Come down to carry water from the spring:
A foe as dangerous as Ekron's King.
And even in the thought, he heard her breath
Drawn quick and deep: that shriek would mean his death!

He moved upon her, heaving high his blade
To strike her dead. But shame and pity stayed
His arm, mid-swing. Was he an Ammonite
To slay a maid? The weapon glittered bright
And keen above her. "Utter but one cry,
And by the God of Israel, thou shalt die!"

With hand on mouth she smothered back the shriek:
It came no louder than a mouse's squeak.
Her piteous eyes had lighted at his vow
With kindling hope. "Of Israel art thou,
And swearest by Jehovah? Then thy blade
Should not be drawn against a Hebrew maid
Held captive by Philistia." "Art thou so?"
He answered her amazed, "I did not know:

MICHMASH

    I had not thought to find upon this steep
    A woman; and bemused with mist and sleep,
    I took thee for a damsel from the den
    Of plundering Philistines. Yet even then,
    I had not drawn against thee, but to save
    My life and his who follows me." He gave
    A glance toward Shammah, who had waked and risen,
    And stood bewildered.

                      "In Mitinti's prison
    We dread not death," she said, "but there are things
    That even a captive fears. Philistia's kings
    Are terrible; but the Amalekite
    Are worse than beasts. And in this shadowy light
    I deemed thee one of them." Then ghastly pale
    She grew, as if a silken milk-white veil
    Were drawn across her face. He marked the weal
    Left by the scorpion with its gads of steel
    Across her shoulder, and he well might guess
    What festering stripes were hidden by her dress.
    Her eyes yet awed him, though her head was bowed
    In shuddering horror, and he groaned aloud
    From pity and a bitter thirst to rest
    Her head upon his shoulder, make a nest
    Of his strong arms, and shield her from the reach
    Of harm. He tried to speak, but found no speech,
    And so stood silent, while his sinewy hand
    Gripped hard upon the pommel of his brand,
    And gnawed his lip, and sware that if the Lord
    But gave him strength, he would not sheathe his sword
    Until he had avenged her. So they stood,
    So still they seemed as figures carved from wood,
    Nor moved nor spake. Meanwhile, the lamp of day
    Brightened, and then was swallowed in the gray
    Of sodden storm-clouds, gathering dark and foul
    Along the eastern heavens: there came a growl

MICHMASH

Of thunder, rumbling like a lion's roar
Before he kills; the crooked lightning tore
The firmament to tatters; then the skies
Grew black again; the wind began to rise
In sobbing gusts.
              She sharply drew her breath
And raised her eyes. "Knowest thou how near to death
Thou art, my lord? I know thee: thou art son
To Saul the King, the noble Jonathan.
What doest thou here? Mitinti, Ekron's Lord,
Hath vowed to comb the land with spear and sword
Until he find thee, tie thee by the heel,
And drag thee bleeding at his chariot's wheel!
And I, God's pity, thinking on my woes,
Have kept thee here, encircled by thy foes.
Oh tarry not! Mitinti's tent is pitched
Upon this rock; his shield, with gold enriched,
Hangs at its entrance, and his dolphin flag
Flies from the topmost rampart of the crag.
Beyond are Hanun, Rusa, Adimar,
With all their hosts, and Amalek's wolves of war
That know no god but plunder, have no joy
Except to kill and torture and destroy,
Are close beside. Mitinti hath decreed
A chariot decked with jewels for the meed
Of him that takes thee captive, and his men
Pant for the prize— It is a lion's den!"

He answered, "I have lifted up my hand
To God, that I will never sheathe my brand
Till I have taken vengeance for thy wrong
On them that wronged thee. One, with God, is strong,
And two are mighty, though their hearts be faint.
For with Jehovah there is no restraint
To save by many, or to save by few.
We will ascend: behold what God will do.

MICHMASH

He hath assured us by most certain signs
That He will give the host of Philistines
This day into our hands. Await thou here
For Israel's deliverance. Be of cheer."

He spake and turned, and Shammah followed him.
Along the ledge there ran a pathway dim,
Now hid by boulders, now along the brink
From which their giddy eyeballs well might shrink,
And then turned sharply upward, through a strait
And sheer-walled passage, like a giant's gate.
Here Jonathan, with pretext to arrange
The trussing of his brigandine, and change
His buckler's brace, ere upward way they took,
Turned to secure one lingering backward look
At fig and fountain, and the captive maid
Yet standing bowed and still, as if she prayed.
His face was iron, but the pounding blood
Within ran ice and fire in mingled flood,
As turning once again the twain addressed
The mounting path, and quickly reached the crest.

V

In other days, a pleasing scene
    Had opened to their view;
For here in Spring the grass was green,
And all its feathery stalks between
    The meadow lilies grew,
And blithely from the fields of corn
The lark's shrill pipe proclaimed the morn
And here had Michmash Village stood,
    With vineyard-lands around,
Fair fields, and clumps of tangled wood,
And olive-yards and orchards good,
    And leagues of pasture ground,

MICHMASH

Where with his flock the shepherd roved,
And thought upon the maid he loved.

But the invader's axe had hewed
Both orchard tree and thorny wood,
And all that nature fashioned fair
   In grass and tree and stone
Wore now a wild and desolate air,
For war's fierce hand had flayed it bare
   And seared it to the bone.
Foot, hoof, and chariot-wheel had marred
The lentil-fields and pasture sward;
The village showed but timbers charred
And hovels roofless and unbarred
   And stones in ruin thrown.

To left, the ridge, by slow descents,
Set thick with Amalek's desert tents,
   Sloped gently toward the west,
And scarce a bow-cast on their right
A blue pavilion crowned the height,
   Mitinti's as they guessed;
For fair before the entrance hung,
As if a challenge proud it flung,
   A gold-emblazoned shield,
And over it a standard flew,
Now half obscured, now plain to view
As fitfully the dawn-wind blew:
Those golden dolphins well they knew
   Upon their azure field.

Below were earthworks, flanked and ditched,
Here tents in martial order pitched,
   With chariots ranked between,
And booths with store of plunder packed,
And tethered steeds, and weapons stacked,
And wains of baggage— Nothing lacked
   To make a warlike scene.

MICHMASH

So much the warriors' roving eyes
At once beheld; and then the skies
   With lightnings blazed amain,
And with their flash, the rising gust
Obscured the camp with driving dust
   As thick as clouds of rain.
They saw Mitinti's regal tent
From pegs ripped loose, with curtains rent,
   To writhe upon the ground,
And as the volleying thunders pealed,
There fell his gold-emblazoned shield
   With sullen, clangorous sound.
And then they saw the dolphin flag
Torn from its staff upon the crag,
   And like an ominous bird
Or broad-vanned demon out of Hell,
Went flapping down the gale, and fell
   Amid the chariot-herd.

Then madly did the horses rear
   And o'er the barriers leap;
With bloodshot eyes aglare with fear,
Through thrashing tents and scattered gear,
   They galloped down the steep.
"Now praise the living Lord of Hosts,"
   Cried Jonathan. "Behold
Our God, that heard their vaunting boasts,
   In dust their power hath rolled!
He overthrows the conqueror's tents
   And breaks the oppressor's rod—
Behold the day of recompense,
   The vengeance of our God!"

And now tumultuous clamor rose:
Some deemed themselves beset by foes,
And cried for bucklers, brands, and bows;

MICHMASH

Some thought upon the scattered spoil,
And others wrought, with fruitless toil,
   To raise their tents again;
Some said that Saul was close at hand;
Some thought the gods that ruled the land
Assailed them with the thunder-brand.
Loud rang the camp with hoarse command
   And furious shouts of men.

Meanwhile, the Prince and Shammah glide
Like phantoms through the dusty shroud
That overspreads the mountainside
Like smoke of burning thorns, or cloud
That holds the thunder, hovering dense
As twilight shades. 'Mid fallen tents
That thrash and billow in the gale,
And plunging steeds, and plunder piled,
And casques and shields and coats of mail
All scattered in confusion wild,
They pick their perilous way; and when
Take form the shadowy shapes of men,
   They hew them to the ground.
And still the furious blows they ply,
Their war-shout bellowing hoarse and high,
The yells of those that fall and die,
   The turmoil worse confound.

Now, shadow-like and dim, appears
To bar their road, a band of spears:
   Mitinti's royal guard;
And in the van a noble shape
With crested helm and purple cape—
   The form of Ekron's lord.
Rings out the Prince's dauntless cry,
   "Jehovah, speed the blow!"
He flings the bull-hide buckler by,

MICHMASH

    With both his hands his blade swings high;
    Like lightning-stroke that cleaves the sky
        It lays Mitinti low.

    Loud rings young Shammah's joyous yell;
    But those who love Mitinti well
    (For with his people, truth to tell,
        A noble name he bore),
    From them there swells a sullen shout
    Where grief is blent with rage and doubt;
    Their eyes flash fire, their swords are out,
        Their pikes thrust straight before:
    And foully Jonathan would fare,
    Unbucklered, and with bosom bare,
        And naught except his blade
    To guard him from a score of brands
    That flash and thrust in furious hands,
        And lances level laid;
    But in the instant comes a shock
    Of earthquake, and the living rock
        Trembles beneath their feet.
    As heaves a galley in the blast,
    When foam-shot waves come rolling fast,
    And chief and seamen stand aghast
        And hearts forget to beat,
    So Michmash Mountain wallows hard
    From crest to base. Mitinti's guard
    Upon each other wondering gaze,
    And wonder deepens to amaze,
        Amaze to panic fright:
    Forgetful of their dying king,
    Upon the ground their arms they fling,
    And terror lends her hurrying wing—
        They go in headlong flight.

    Now all around there rose a cry
    That fiends below and gods on high
        Against Philistia warred;

That Amalek's desert warriors broke
On their allies with treacherous stroke,
   And Saul beset them hard.
Still shook the ridge with earthquake throes,
And cliff and crag and woodland reeled,
While louder still the tumult rose
Where friends fought friends and deemed them foes;
Groans, imprecations, insults, blows,
   And clash of spear on shield.

VI

The shock that staggered Michmash steep
Waked Saul the King from troubled sleep;
Although at Gibeah, less profound,
The earthquake gently heaved the ground,
As freshening sea-swells softly sway
The galleys on a sheltered bay,
While tempest-driven surges shout
In foam on barrier reefs without.
But yet it waked him: o'er his head
The tall pomegranate bent and swayed,
And tossed its red and russet fruit,
Though whether from the earthquake-jar
That heaved the ground about its root,
Or from the wind that levied war
Against the rack of scudding cloud
That raced through heaven, he did not know.
He heard drums beat and trumpets blow,
That blent with rumbling sounds afar,
Now swelling into tumult loud,
Now faint and muffled like the hum
Of hiving bees, or sinking low
Almost to silence— Then the drum,
The trumpet-peal, the clash of blade
In furious strife on buckler laid
Swelled into pandemonium.

MICHMASH

He rose, and something like to fear
Tugged at his heart. Was Abner near,
And Jethir, and the faithful few
That still behind him weapons drew?
   Or had they left him, all?
Let him that ne'er from slumber woke
To earthquake-shock and battle-stroke
And thought of God's commandment broke,
   Give judgment on King Saul!

But now came Jethir to his side,
With eyes in wonder opened wide;
"My lord, my lord the King!" he cried,
   "A marvel is begun.
All Michmash Ridge is thick with dust
And loud with trump and battle-thrust:
They are beset with foes, we trust,
   Come, see what there is done."

He led his master to a crest
Where Abner was, and all the rest;
   And thence they might behold
Beyond the gorge the dusty cloud
That, swelling with a tumult loud,
   Round Michmash Mountain rolled.

While yet they looked in wondering awe,
And scarce could credit what they saw,
The wind that raised the dust-cloud dark
   Lifted it from the field,
And for a moment they could mark
The hilltop strewn with ruin stark
   In open day revealed.
The heart of Saul beat high with hope,
For all on Michmash height and slope
   The conflict raged amain.
Though dimmed by distance was the sight,

They saw Philistia's bucklers bright
And Amalek's spears and turbans white,
In mingled combat, rout and flight,
    Roll slowly toward the plain.

And even the spoilers in the field
    The mad contagion caught,
For far and wide the turmoil reeled,
Where Philistines did furious wield
Their blades on Midian's bull-hide shield,
    Not knowing whom they fought,
And Amalek's lances thrust and broke
Through Moab's ranks, with level stroke,
    And wild confusion wrought.
A little space they watched the fight;
Then pelting raindrops blurred the sight.

But ill the mind of Saul could brook
To tarry for the time it took
To number and equip his band
With weapons such as lay at hand—
A brigandine, a pike, a brand,
A sickle or a pruning-hook,
Javelin and helmet, carried back
From Phicol's rout or Geba's sack,
A goad, an axe, a dart, a sling—
With such mixed weapons must the King
His warriors to the battle bring.
And yet, although in number few,
And ill equipped, their hearts were stout;
And when for march the trumpet blew
    A hearty cheer rang out,
That shook the mountains' wild defiles,
The caverns and the forest aisles,
    And at the thunderous shout
The Hebrews hid in cave and den
Came forth and joined the marching men.

MICHMASH

Though paths were steep, and thickly sown
With ruin by the earthquake strown;
Though dust was changed to clinging mud,
And torrents swift, in seething flood
Through all the rocky hollows raced,
Yet, spurred by hope to fiery haste,
Their march was swift. Ere mid of morn
They halted in a wood forlorn
Of juniper and scraggly thorn
　That skirted Michmash Hill;
And soon the foe, through dripping rain,
Came straggling forth upon the plain,
　In wild confusion still;
Though rage and fear began to wane,
And leaders labored, not in vain,
Some show of order to regain.

Here, unsuspecting of the snare,
The trumpets took them unaware:
　Fresh panic seized them all;
Then came the assault. No need to speak
Of Saul in arms! His kindling cheek
And glaring eyes, the flash of blade
That lightning-like around him played—
　These made the name of Saul
A terror. And they wist not yet
With what a power they were beset:
　Though some turned back to fight,
They fought despairing and in vain,
And deemed the sound of pelting rain
The tramp of hosts. By thousands slain
They fell, or wildly sought to gain
　Safety in craven flight.

Long did the Hebrew minstrels tell
The rout and slaughter that befell,
And how, before the set of sun,
The fight rolled down to Aijalon;

But, for the sin that Saul had done,
He could not break Philistia's power.
By night, the remnant of their host,
Their baggage and their chariots lost,
Regained their cities on the coast,
   And there abode their hour.

Amalek

I

Amalek dwelt in the desert
  Where the scant, gray thorn-trees grew,
And the shadeless, shimmering hills of sand
Stretched far and away on every hand
  To a sky-rim burning and blue.

Amalek's cheeks were swarthy,
  Amalek's beard was curled;
His lips were thick and his loins were lean,
His soul was black and bitter and mean,
  And his hand was against the world.

Amalek turned no furrow,
  Amalek sowed no seed:
With crooked sabers he did his reaping
Where men were dying and women weeping,
  And Amalek knew no need.

Amalek's trade was pillage,
  Torture was Amalek's boast;
He bought his bread with his crooked blade,
And he hated all men that the Lord had made,
  But he hated Israel most.

When Israel came from Egypt,
  Faint with the dust of the way,
Amalek cut off the weary and old
And butchered the babe in its mother's hold
  And bore off their maids for his prey.

AMALEK

But Moses, with Hur and Aaron,
   Went up and stood on the height,
And prayed to the Lord with uplifted hands,
While Joshua smote the Amalekite bands
   From morn till the dusk of the night.

And Moses wrote up for remembrance,
   That all generations might heed,
How God had made oath by the might of His hand
To blot the Amalekite out of the land,
   And leave them not remnant nor seed.

Yet Amalek still was mighty,
   He mocked at Jehovah's ban.
His joy was slaughter, his god was plunder;
His spears were lightning, his hoofs were thunder;
   He feared not the face of man.

Amalek was a devil,
   Implacable, sullen, accursed:
He knew not wonder, nor song, nor mirth,
And he hated all men on the face of the earth,
   But he hated Israel worst.

II

Now came God's word to Samuel, "Lo, the King
   I set o'er Israel hath turned aside
   From My commands, to walk in sullen pride
And all his evil heart's imagining.

"Yet I will try him once again, and find
   If he repent and wholly do my will,
   Or if he be perverse and wayward still,
And walk according to his stubborn mind.

"Go then, and bid him this that I command:
   That he perform the oath I sware the day
   When Amalek met my people in the way,
To blot his name forever from the land.

AMALEK

"Yet see thou warn him not, nor bid him go,
  Nor add to my command the smallest word;
  But let thy message be, 'Thus saith the Lord,'
And see if he will do my will or no."

Now Saul was camped near Sorek, in the vale,
  While Israel gathered spoil and stripped the dead
  Along the way Philistia's host had fled,
And all his men were armed with spears and mail.

And many had returned to field and tent,
  But Saul yet tarried, wishing to attack
  Philistia's borders, waste her fields, and sack
Her cities, if the Lord would give consent.

Then Samuel came, and spake before the face
  Of Saul the King: "Thus saith the Lord of Hosts,
  'When Israel came forth from Egypt's coasts
To take his journey to the promised place,

"'I marked what Amalek did: how he withstood
  My people's march, assailed their camp by night,
  And slew the infant in its mother's sight
And left the elders groaning in their blood.

"'Now therefore,' saith the Lord, 'Go thou, and keep
  The oath I sware, and blot from out my sight
  All that pertain to the Amalekite,
Man, woman, suckling, camel, ox and sheep.'"

And as he spake, the Prophet marked the blood
  Leap red in Saul's dark face, and knew the thought
  That lurked behind: "The victory I wrought
Hath made the Lord repent his sullen mood.

"He knoweth no hand like mine to wield the sword,
  Nor voice to cheer the laggards in the fight:
  Who else can pour on the Amalekite
The long-withholden vengeance of the Lord?

AMALEK

"He seeks my favor, seeing how I trod
   The Philistines like grass, and how my blade
   Hewed down their mighty ones without his aid:
God hath more need of me than I of God."

So thought the King; and Samuel read his mind
   As learned men the letters on a scroll
   Surcharged with lamentation and with dole,
And in his heart he groaned, "O deaf and blind!"

He yearned to warn him—tell how he had wrung
   This grace from God by long and piteous prayer,
   And naught remained but madness and despair
If here he failed—but God had tied his tongue.

He might not speak one little word: his lips
   Were sealed alike to warn or to implore,
   Though well he knew what ruin lay before,
God's vengeance poured in thunder and eclipse.

And he had loved the King as his own son;
   For him had gladly stripped himself of power:
   Was this the end—to see him, in one hour,
By folly base and willful pride undone?

His thought went slipping back to that far day
   When first he met the man: he had been vexed
   With grief for his rejection, and perplexed
With waiting on the Lord. The dusk grew gray,

While tarrying yet he watched the people going
   With shouts and laughter to the sacrifice;
   Again he saw the altar-smoke arise,
And heard far timbrels played and trumpets blowing.

And then this youth had come; and he had known him,
   At that first look, for God's appointed King,
   And he had heard far choirs of angels sing,
"Behold the man! Anoint him and enthrone him!"

AMALEK

Then, rapt with hope, he had beheld a splendid
   And wondrous vision, lighting that drab hour—
   God's Kingdom, in its majesty and power,
His will on earth made law; oppression ended.

All this flashed through the Prophet's mind; the vision
   Of what Saul was, and what he might have been—
   This prince of men, too blind to see his sin—
Oh, grief of Paradise, and Hell's derision!

And in the moment did his pity turn
   To fiery indignation for the man
   That once he loved, whose hands had marred the plan
Of God Most High. His gentle face grew stern,

His look flashed flames of fire; he seemed to rise
   To giant stature, and the monarch felt
   His heart grow faint, his bones within him melt
Before the anger in the Prophet's eyes.

And twice the old man lifted up his hand
   To pour the curse of God upon his head,
   And twice the imprecation died unsaid:
He was not sent to curse, but to command.

The fire had died, and left him cold as stone,
   Forspent and trembling with the fury past:
   "The Lord hath spoken, Saul," he said at last,
And slowly turned, and left the King alone.

And now, indeed, the spirits that are sent
   To warn the soul, and turn it from the verge
   Of its eternal death, began to scourge
The King with scorpions, bidding him repent

Of his offenses, and no more to harden
   His bitter heart, but while it was to-day,
   Turn back from all the evil of his way
And pledge obedience and sue for pardon.

AMALEK

Sweet memories came of benefits conferred,
   Of strength in battle, comfort in distress,
   Wife, child, and friend to share his loneliness,
Fresh hope in failure, counsel when he erred;

God's choice of him as King, when but a youth
   Unproved in war or peace; His guiding hand
   Through years when dark oppression trod the land;
The promise of the kingdom, now proved truth.

And then the certainty that he had failed
   In courage and obedience, and that spite
   Toward Samuel, more than zeal for Israel's right,
Had moved him to that deed, his soul assailed;

Till, overcome by anguish, he abhorred
   The pettiness and malice of his soul,
   And longing of that sickness to be whole,
He all but cried for mercy to the Lord.

And then, like demons whimpering in a wind
   That blows among the tombs, all falsehoods hid,
   And every evil deed he ever did,
Arose and cried, "Yield not: thou hast not sinned!"

He wished the Seer had tarried for a space,
   Till he found words to prick his overblown
   Self-righteousness: he would have made him own
The fault was his, and shamed him to his face,

Recounting all the wrongs he had endured
   From God and Samuel—for he held them one—
   Defeats and disappointments undergone,
Deep wounds of flesh and spirit yet uncured;

Long marches, thirst and hunger by the way,
   The promise of the crown so long delayed
   Nor yet performed; his lovely, star-eyed maid
Snatched from him, all but on his marriage-day.

AMALEK

What help did God afford him, when he chased
   The desert robbers through their land accursed
   Of sand and thorns, and almost died of thirst,
And lost their trail upon the wind-blown waste?

And it was Amalek—or so at least
   The King believed—that seized upon his love
   As leaps the sneaking weasel on the dove
To suck her blood. That snarling desert beast

Had borne her to his horrid den, subdued
   Her milk-white body to his lawless lust,
   Dragged down her flaming spirit to the dust,
And made her bear and nurse his hateful brood.

Oh why had God remembered not his vow
   In that dark hour, before the hope was past
   Of saving her from horror that must last
While life endured— Or why recall it now?

Far better he should see her not again
   Than find her starry beauty withered there,
   Grown foul and bestial in a filthy lair,
A savage mother of more savage men.

But had he asked the counsel of the Seer,
   Or offered sacrifice, or sought the help
   Of God, ere he pursued that devil's whelp?
Nay, he had trusted in his bow and spear.

So furiously did tides of conflict roll
   Across Saul's mind, at once the prize and place
   Of combat, where the ugliest and most base
Made war with what was noblest in his soul:

Dark malice, envy, anger, petty spite,
   And puffy pride and sneering mockery warred
   With honest faith, allegiance to the Lord,
And love of justice and the zeal for right.

AMALEK

And in the end of all, the King attained
  But half-repentance: he would do the part
  Assigned by God, but with a grudging heart;
His bitterness of spirit yet remained.

III

The King marched south across a withering world;
War-wasted fields, grown strangers to the plough
Or foot of man; bare woods, where dry leaves whirled
Or clung despondent to the lifeless bough:
The naked pastures were deserted now
Of flock and herd; the Autumn's flags were furled.

He gave his regal ensign to the air
Above the sandy hills of Telaim
In Simeon's utmost borders, mustering there
His hosts for war, along the desert's rim.
The heavens rolled blue and umber over him;
The wilderness before stretched white and bare.

Here lay the land of the Amalekite
As far as eye could see: the barren home
Of ostrich and of dragon, shimmering white
As wintry snow or ocean's shaggy foam,
Unchanged since first creation, with her dome
Of stars, had issued from the womb of night.

On Simeon's coast the King arrayed his band
While Autumn, smouldering twilight of the year,
Burned low—ten thousand men that drew the brand,
Two hundred thousand more that drave the spear
He mustered there; then trumpets sounding clear
Proclaimed the march on Amalek's desolate land.

Meantime, through Benjamin's untrodden ways,
Did Jonathan and Shammah exiled roam,
Dishonored outlaws, while the Autumn days

AMALEK

Went sounding down the year, with gleam and gloam
On withered woodland and unfurrowed loam,
Dim sun, and silver shower, and shadowy haze.

For on that morning when the trumpeting
Of wind and thunder on Philistia burst,
And Israel gathered for pursuit, the King,
Before the trumpets blew assault, had cursed
That man who turned aside to quench his thirst
Or stay his hunger ere the evening.

But Jonathan, who in the vanguard hewed,
(For he was absent when his father bound
The people with the oath) as he pursued
The fliers through Beth-aven's woodland, found
A stream of honey dripping to the ground
From storm-rent oak, and tasted of the food.

And, as it often haps that they who break
The laws most lightly are the first to blame
When other men transgress, as if to make
Their own offenses less by crying *shame*,
Invoke the honor of the law, and claim
A swift requital by the noose or stake,

So now it was with Saul; for when he learned
Of Jonathan's transgression, he had vowed
The Prince should die the death his trespass earned;
But straightway all the people cried aloud,
"Shall Jonathan be slain, who hath endowed
Our hearts with hope, and shame to victory turned?"

And by main might they rescued Jonathan,
And saved him from the merciless decree
Of death: yet had the King pronounced the ban
Upon his son, that he henceforth should see
No more his father's favor, and should be
Cut off from kind and kin, a banished man.

AMALEK

Thus Jonathan a wanderer became
Of wild, unpeopled wastes, with none for friend
But Shammah: faithful in the hour of shame
As that of victory, he would attend
His master's steps until the world should end,
And share his exile and his evil fame.

What matter where they went? The King had banned
All those that sheltered them or bade them speed:
They were become as strangers in the land
Of their nativity; and this their meed
For victory won—that they should be indeed
Accursed from men; for such was Saul's command.

And yet, the bitterness of his disgrace,
More poignant that the Prince had looked for praise,
Not wholly blurred the memory of a face
That, seen but once, still lit his dreary days,
Like visioned streams and palm trees, that amaze
The sun-parched wanderer in a desert place.

And so they lingered in Beth-aven's wood,
Half hoping that the King might yet relent,
And lived on game they hunted as they could,
And roots and honey; while the Autumn spent
Her hoard of golden days. But Saul had sent
No word of pardon; so the sentence stood.

Then came a time when from the rocky heights
The beacons flamed, and trumps were sounding wide,
While posts went racing northward: there were sights
To stir a warrior's soul, as that great tide
Of Israel's arms, now twice in battle tried
And proved, rolled down on the Amalekites.

Then spake the Prince, "O Shammah, I abhor
My very life. God knows, if I had done
A sin, I would not shun to die therefor

AMALEK

Or suffer banishment; but there was none.
Far better I had never seen the sun,
Than hide my face while Israel strives in war."

And Shammah answered, "In a noble mind
No shame should spring from punishment unjust.
Magnanimous and kingly souls may find
The joy of battle in misfortune's thrust:
Nor should the Prince of Israel sit in dust
And cloth of hair, because the law is blind."

And Jonathan made answer, "Thou wast born
A bondman, Shammah, yet thy words have shamed
Thy master. Worthier art thou to adorn,
Than I, the scroll where mighty kings are named.
My spirit shall not sit in ashes, maimed,
Because my father held me up to scorn."

Then Shammah said, "What wilt thou do, my lord?
The game grows scarce, and we are like to die
Of hunger. Zobah's King might use thy sword;
Or Tadmor, where the caravans go by
To Nineveh; or Tyre, that doth defy
Great ocean, with her galleys hundred-oared."

The Prince replied, "This Midianitish brand
My father won in battle, long ago,
At risk of life. He placed it in my hand
To smite for Israel; nor will I go
And sell its stroke to strangers, friend or foe,
But draw it only for my native land.

"It yet may be that by the Lord's good will
My father's love shall turn to me again.
Then let it find me ready to fulfill
His bidding as of old. And until then,
Though hiding beastlike, let us live as men,
Held faithful to the King's commandment still.

AMALEK

"Thou seest the land lies naked: all the strong
Are gone to war with Amalek. It may be
That foes who have oppressed our land so long,
Not wholly beaten yet, may think they see
In this occasion opportunity
To strike again, and do us deeper wrong.

"I know a rocky den near Gibeah, where
We may find shelter, and from thence keep guard
Upon the hold. For likely none are there
To keep the place but boys, not yet grown hard,
And graybeard shepherds, in old battles scarred:
There may be much to do, and much to dare.

"And if we hunger, if we suffer pain,
Toil, peril, weariness and thirst and cold,
The certain loss, the most uncertain gain—
Have we not suffered these full oft of old?
They were our portion. Let us, then, be bold;
And if we die, my father yet shall reign."

The twain turned eastward, by the ways that led
Toward Gibeah, where so late the steel had hewn
Among Philistia's nobles while they fled:
Hushed was the tumult, but the land was strewn
With broken weapons, and—a horrid boon
To kite and wolf—the yet unburied dead.

The Prince moved on as one that dreams, immersed
In reveries of the damsel on the cleft.
Though hope of finding her he scarcely nursed,
Yet still her memory, like a golden weft,
Shot through his somber musings: had she left
His thought one instant, since he saw her first?

And when his comrade spake of glories done—
How here the foe had rallied; here they broke
And fled; there fought the King of Ashkelon

AMALEK

With Abner's men; here Saul had dealt that stroke
On Rusa's shield—he answered not, or spoke
But words at random found, and hastened on.

They clomb the slope of Michmash from the west,
Yet foul with carnage. These no more would gird
The sword for war, nor lay the spear in rest.
On all the ridge was death, and nothing stirred
But furtive jackals, and the carrion bird
That flapped and croaked above the warrior's breast.

The Prince thought not of them, and yet these too
Had loves, no doubt, and many a maid would weep
In strange, far cities, where the curling blue
Fell frothing down the shores; and wives would sleep
Alone. And these yet lay like murrained sheep,
While over them the carrion eagles flew.

All have their griefs, and each must mourn his own.
The heart, engrossed in its pale cup of tears,
Sits sorrowing on the altar-stairs alone
And drinks its bitter brew; and if it hears
The anguish of creation beat its ears,
It deems it but its own sad monotone.

Here ran the path: he must be nigh the spot
Where he had left the maid. He thought how bare
The place must be without her: tremblings shot
Through all his frame. Oh yet would linger there
Some warm, sweet ghost of her? Or would despair
Be doubly dark, that here he found her not?

How desolate and sad those places are
Where love hath been, but now is found no more!
How nigh the feet, but from the soul how far!
The shadowy lane, the garden by the shore,
The vacant room with dust upon the floor,
The rustling grove beneath the evening star.

AMALEK

These are the holy places of the heart,
The secret shrines. Thou, Grief, dost keep the gate
In silence. Barren Memory, thou art
Sole oracle. The votary, soon or late,
Comes stealing back to worship and to wait,
And bow the head, and silently depart.

He found the ledge, once hallowed by her tread,
The fig, now bare of foliage, that had heard
The beating of her heart, and all she said.
The Prince rehearsed in mind each simple word
She spake to him, and how her mantle stirred
Above her breast, and how she bowed her head.

Her presence lingered like a smell of myrrh:
Almost he saw her now beside the spring,
Vague loveliness, but wavering through a blur
Of sudden tears. Could any magic bring
Peace to his heart again? He might be king
Of all the earth, yet poor for want of her.

Then, like a blight, the recollection came,
He knew not who she was, nor where she dwelt.
Ah, cursèd folly, not to ask her name!
Nor would the chance return, although he knelt
In prayer forever: his own hand had dealt
That sorry stroke: none other was to blame.

One hope remained: it might be she had fled
To Gibeah for safety, since the land
Was overrun with beasts, and tenanted,
He knew, by many a roving outlaw band,
That now, unchecked by Saul's avenging hand,
Would bolder wax, and fill the ways with dread.

And Gibeah must be all but undefended!
The maddening thought aroused the Prince to haste.
He gave the word, and swiftly they descended

AMALEK

    The eastward ramp; the fading day they raced
    Toward home; and saw the walls of Gibeah traced
    Against the darkening sky, ere day had ended.

    Familiar scene! And yet the Prince's mind
    Misgave him: was it home? Was this the field
    Where Saul had taught his infant hands to bind
    The barley-sheaves? Had here his hurts been healed
    By mother-care? Here had he learnt to yield
    Obedience to a father rough yet kind?

    No home was here for him: a man exiled,
    To whom the faces of his friends were changed,
    By all men shunned, as if he were defiled
    With leprosy; from help and hope estranged,
    Abhorred and hated, like a beast that ranged
    Through lonely woods and kenneled in the wild.

    He once was welcome there— How long ago!
    There dwelt Ahinoam, his gentle mother:
    Would she disown him, who had loved him so?
    And would his sisters and his younger brother
    Hold him in hatred now? ... And was that other
    Dear face among them there? He might not know.

    For even though they loved him, they would keep
    The King's command. However he might plead,
    They would not answer him. The very sheep
    That in far days and dear he used to lead
    Would flee from him in fear—or so indeed
    It seemed to him, his anguish being deep.

    And yet, if he might know his love was safe,
    How gladly could he suffer infamy
    And thirst and hunger! Yea, he would not chafe—
    Or so he told himself—though he must flee
    As felons fly from all their kind, and be
    To life's dark end an outlaw and a waif.

AMALEK

He must not ask her love, although it wrung
His heart, not yet her pity if he died.
He would not have her grieve, though he were stung
With every anguish. He would put aside
All hope of her...all hope...and though he lied,
He yet believed it wholly, being young.

Oh Youth, oh happy Youth! Thy very grief
Is gilded with a gleam that sober Age
Finds not in his chief joy: for Time, the thief,
Hath robbed us of our golden heritage,
And left us toiling for a meagre wage
Of musty wine and scant and mildewed sheaf.

Oh Youth! oh bitter Youth! Thy joys most dear
Are tinged with somber musings; and the dark
Is unto noonday's golden splendor near.
For thee the owlet's cry, the fox's bark
Are roars of far-off lions; and the lark,
Twittering through Autumn rain, thou canst not hear.

"Abide," said Jonathan, "and I will steal
More near the place. For while the world is cloaked
In twilight, I may learn my mother's weal
Or peril. Though my sentence unrevoked
Hath closed the doors against me—" Here he choked
With grief, and sharply turned upon his heel.

He knew the rugged path, and through the gloam
Went slipping like a shadow down the steep.
The air dripped sweetness like a honeycomb,
And in the firmament, grown blue and deep,
Astarte lit her pallid lamp. The sheep
Were folded for the night; the herds were home.

He crossed the vineyards, bare of leaves, and browned
By Autumn's touch: then came an olive-yard,
With tillage land between; and here he found,

AMALEK

    Issuing upon it, that his way was barred
    By one in armor keeping lonely guard,
    A single warrior, with a helmet crowned.

    He knew him: Doeg, called the Edomite,
    A man of scanty words and heavy blows,
    Well skilled to swing the sword and make it bite
    Through casque and skull; a terror unto foes
    And dangerous to friends; most apt to close
    At once, nor stay to parley ere he smite.

    Here lay a lion in the way! The hold
    Was not unguarded. What a witless fool
    He was, to dream his father—very mould
    Of strategy, and master in the school
    Of mountain war—would break its simplest rule,
    And leave no dog unchained to watch his fold!

    Half glad he was, half sorry. For her sake—
    The nameless maid's—he deemed that he could strive
    Lone-handed with the Philistines, and break
    The teeth of lions; yea, that he could drive
    Moab and Ammon to their desert hive,
    And make the fiery heart of Midian quake.

    But still, he had no wish to deal in blows
    With Doeg. He had seen the bondman leap
    Upon a lion, smite it on the nose
    With but a shepherd's staff, and take the heap
    Of mangled flesh that once had been a sheep
    From out its jaws, as one might pluck a rose.

    Besides, though outlawed, he would keep the law:
    He would not cross his father's will, nor brawl
    With those that served him; neither would he draw
    His sword against them. Though his heart was gall
    And wormwood, he was yet the son of Saul,
    And held the King in honor and in awe.

AMALEK

To pass the Edomite was not so hard
For one that knew the ground, although at cost
Of regal bearing: stealthy as a pard
He slipped from shade to shadow; so he crossed
The field unseen by Doeg, and was lost
Among the shadows of the olive-yard.

The gray leaves whispered; yonder ran the stream
Where he had played in childhood. Could he bear
Its friendly murmur now, its silver gleam? . . .
What mystic presence filled the hallowed air
With loveliness? Was someone standing there
Beside the rock-hewn pool? Or did he dream?

Through such a twilight, not of dusk but dawn,
By such a pool, he had beheld that shape,
Slim loveliness that quivered like a fawn
That sees the huntsman come, and finds escape
Cut off: he knew those eyes, that hooded cape—
If he were dreaming, might he yet dream on!

She was not trembling now, nor had she stirred,
Although she saw and knew him. Now from some
Leaf-shadowed olive-bough a hidden bird
Twittered his vesper-psalm, and then was dumb.
The dusk drew close around them. "Hast thou come?"
Her deep eyes questioned, but she spake no word.

Where now, O Jonathan, thy holy vows?
Thou hast abjured her: she is not for thee.
Look not upon her loveliness; arouse
Thine honor! Thou art outlawed: wouldst thou be
Foresworn, my Prince? O twilight witchery!
O twittering bird, and whispering olive-boughs!

A fig for vows! Youth was not made to reap
Among the tombs! It is the twilight hour.
Let honor hang himself! The blood must leap,

AMALEK

    The flesh rejoice, and love unfold its flower,
    Though ravenous Time sit waiting to devour
    The opening bud, when deep cries unto deep.

    Her head is on his shoulder. Flash and foam,
    Thou little stream! Whisper, ye olive leaves!
    Drip down your sweetness like a honeycomb,
    O soft and dewy heavens, while Beauty weaves
    Her golden web of stars; for love receives
    Its own again, and Jonathan is home.

IV

    Saul hath broken Amalek,
        Saul the King!
    Set his heel on Agag's neck,
        Saul the King!
    Joyful let the damsels sing,
    And their arms with gems bedeck,
        Sound the pipe and pluck the string:
    Saul hath broken Amalek,
        Saul the King.

    Saul hath slaughtered man and woman,
        Saul the King!
    Ox and camel, beast and human,
        Saul the King!
    He returns from journeying:
    Let no grief our gladness check;
        Pour the wine, the fatlings bring!
    Saul hath broken Amalek,
        Saul the King!

    Saul hath taken with his spear,
        Saul the King,
    Agag, whom we held in fear;
        Saul the King!
    Agag knows a secret thing,

AMALEK

    Therefore is his blood unshed:
        For a ransom let him bring
    Her whom Saul betrothed to wed—
        Saul the King!

    Saul hath brought a spoil of flocks,
        Saul the King!
    Lowing heifer, bellowing ox;
        Saul the King.
      At the altar of the Lord
    Let him immolate them all,
        And their blood, for sin outpoured,
    Shall atonement make for Saul—
        Saul the King!

So Saul returned from war; and all the ways
Were thronged with folk that shouted loud his praise.

He came to Gilgal, where he would disband
His host; and thither Samuel came to stand
Before the King; and Saul arose, and made
Obeisance, saying, "Lo, I have obeyed
Thy God's commandments, and am come again
In peace, from overthrow of Agag's men."

And Samuel answered him, "If these be words
Of truth, what mean the lowing of the herds
And bleating of the flocks? Was this a day
To gather spoil, or to lay waste and slay?"

And Saul said, "Yea, I did the Lord's command,
And blotted Amalek from out his land;
Nor yet did I transgress in anything,
But smote them unto Shur, and brought their king
A captive. And the people took the spoil,
That they might offer flesh, with wine and oil,
To God, from whom this triumph we enjoyed;
And all the rest we utterly destroyed."

AMALEK

>   Then Samuel questioned, "Was not this thy mind?
>   Through disobedience thou didst hope to find
>   Thy love; and therefore thou hast saved alive
>   The chief and king of all this shameful hive,
>   This woman-stealer, one that keeps not faith
>   With man or God: thou savedst him from death
>   For thine own ends. But if thou hadst obeyed
>   The words of God, thou wouldst have found the maid
>   At Gath. For thither did this desert beast
>   Take her, and sold her unto Dagon's priest.
>   There yet she dwells; and hadst thou kept the law,
>   Behold, the Philistines had been as straw
>   For thee to thresh, and thou hadst trod them down,
>   And made their cities jewels for thy crown.
>   Saul, I have loved thee; and I know thee bold
>   And high of heart; but thou this day hast sold
>   Thy soul for ashes. They that serve the Lord
>   Must serve in darkness, and obey His word
>   Though seeing not the end."

                              Saul turned away
And bowed his head; but Samuel bade him, "Stay,
That I may tell thee what this night the Lord
Hath said to me." As one who feels a sword
Twist in the wound before it is withdrawn,
Saul turned again, and answered him, "Say on."

"Behold," the Prophet said, "when thou wast small
In thine own eyes and in the eyes of all,
Was it not God that chose thee for the head
Of all His tribes? And He discomfited
Thy foes before thee, and hath made thee great.
And when thou wast established in thy gate,
He sent thee on a journey, saying, 'Fight
Against the sinners, the Amalekite,
And blot them from the earth, which they have cursed
With deeds of blood and treachery, since first

AMALEK

They walked upon it.' Wherefore hast thou flown
Upon the spoil, and saved it for thine own,
When God bade thee destroy it? Thou didst sin
And disobey the Lord."

                      Saul asked, "Wherein
Is mine offending? I have gone the way
Jehovah sent me, and have brought this day
King Agag captive; and the people brought
An offering to Jehovah, as they ought."

But Samuel answered, "Doth the Lord delight
In offerings, or in them that keep aright
His high commandments? Thou hast yet to learn
That to obey is better than to burn
A thousand rams. Thou hast despised and trod
His counsels underfoot. And so hath God
Rejected thee as King, and chosen now
Thy neighbor, that is worthier than thou."

So saying, he turned to go; but Saul laid hold
Upon the Prophet's mantle, and its fold
Was rent apart; and Saul cried out, "Yet stay,
O Man of God! Forgive my sin, I pray."
And Samuel said, "So is thy kingdom rent:
The Strength of Israel will not repent
Nor lie, nor waver, nor recall His word.
Behold, thou art rejected of the Lord."

But ere he went, the Prophet bade them bring
Before him Agag; and the captive king
Came smiling in his beard, and saying, "Lo,
The bitterness of death is past: I know
The King hath sworn me life." "But one more high
Than he in power, hath sworn that thou shalt die,"
The Prophet said; whereat he took a sword
And hewed the man to shreds before the Lord,

AMALEK

  And said, "O Agag, as thy crooked blade
And spear have many mothers childless made,
So is thy mother childless!" Then he gave
The sword to Saul, and bade them dig a grave
In that same spot, and bury him from sight
That once was King of the Amalekite.

  And with this saying did the Seer depart
For Rama; and the King, with heavy heart,
Dismissed his soldiery, and so returned
To Gibeah of Saul. And there he yearned
For Jonathan his son; and by and by,
Being but flesh and blood, he sent a cry
Through all the realm, that by the King's good grace
Prince Jonathan again might see his face.

  So Jonathan returned, and so the King
Forgave him graciously. And in the Spring
When birds made nests among the flowery thorn,
(She having lands, and being nobly born)
The Prince was wedded to his gentle maid
And loved her tenderly.

       And Saul arrayed
His hosts for war, and led them forth, and fought
With all that troubled Israel; and he wrought
Great victories, and made himself a name
Renowned in war and peace.

       But Samuel came
No more to Saul until his life was done,
But mourned for him, as for an only son.

David

I

Now on the day when Jonathan was wed,
   The man of God had gone to Bethlehem
To consecrate another in the stead
   Of Saul. But, fearful lest the King condemn
     His deed, he went by stealth,
And all in secrecy ordained that one
Whom God had chosen, David, Jesse's son,
   Anointing him that he should reign as King
     Of Israel's commonwealth.

The lad was but a stripling. Ruddy locks
   Curled round his brows, and he was fair of eyes,
Yet hard and strong from following the flocks,
   Deep-browned by wind and sun and open skies;
     And sweetly could he play
The shepherd's harp, and pluck the zither's string,
And blow the syrinx, and could make and sing
   The simple pastoral, the sacred psalm,
     And the heroic lay.

His father's elder sons had followed Saul
   To fight with Agag: they could talk of war,
Strange scenes and camps and marches; they were tall
   And bearded, and Eliab showed a scar,
     (Although it was not deep)

DAVID

    And all could boast of having seen the King.
    They held young David but an underling,
      A child, unfit to mingle in their talk,
      And made him keep the sheep.

    Yet David's dreams were filled with mighty deeds
      Of valor. He had made himself a bow
    Of juniper, and shafts from slender reeds,
      And practiced with them on the hawk and crow;
      And he could sling a stone
    At forty strides, and strike within a span,
    With force to knock the breath from out a man,
      Or drive a leopard howling home, or crack
      A lion's frontal bone.

    And many a lay he made to celebrate
      The deeds of prowess that the King had done:
    How he had driven Nahash from the gate
      Of Jabesh Gilead; how he fought and won
      Against tremendous odds
    The battle with Philistia's haughty host,
    And rolled them back from Michmash to the coast,
      To sit in ashes at their temple-gates
      And wail before their gods.

    But most he loved to sing of Jonathan:
      His victory over Phicol at Beth-aven,
    And how he slaughtered Geba's garrison
      And made their flesh a banquet for the raven;
      How, in Philistia's teeth,
    He scaled the Crag of Bozez, and the Lord
    Unsheathed above his head the lightning-sword,
      Let loose the whirlwind, blotted out the sky,
      And shook the earth beneath.

    Or he himself would fight the Philistines
      In mummery, clambering up some rocky cliff

On hands and knees, exulting if the spines
   Of brambles tore him, or his limbs grew stiff
      As Jonathan's had done;
And when he reached the top, with sudden shout
Of onset, he would fiercely lay about,
   With staff for weapon, at the thistle-stalks,
      And slay them one by one.

Yet he was gentle: death he did not love
   Nor cruelty. It was the flash and pride
Of war that moved him. If he shot a dove
   His heart reproached his hand, and when it died
      He smoothed its irised wings
And mourned its beauty, making soft lament
That life should be so brief, his instrument
   Filling the intervals with whimpering notes
      Struck off from muted strings.

In short, he was a simple-hearted boy,
   Whose soul bowed down in worship of the King
As youth alone can worship, and whose joy
   Was ever in the hope that he might bring
      Some gift of service fine
To him he honored: fling himself between
The Lord's anointed and the weapons keen,
   And take their bitter thrust; and hear him say,
      "He gave his life for mine."

And Jonathan would fix his pitying eyes
   Upon him, as he lay incarnadined
With oozing blood, and whisper, "Lo, he dies;
   And none so noble hath he left behind!"
      And Saul's fair daughters then,
Tall Merab, slender Michal, they would mourn
And wring their hands, to see him homeward borne,
   And cry, "Alas, alas! We shall not look
      Upon his like again!"

DAVID

    Yet, though he lived in dreams, the lad could dare
      In hour of need, and he was swift to do
  In peril: if a lion or a bear
      Took from his flock a lamb, he would pursue
        The spoiler to his den
With sling and brandished staff, no whit in awe
Of snarls or snapping teeth or ripping claw,
    And he would spoil the robber of his prey
      And fetch it home again.

Now, on the day that Samuel called him near
    And hallowed him, he did not tell the reason,
But said, "The Lord hath chosen thee to hear
    And do his will." And since it had been treason
      To deem he should be King,
All those beholding thought the oil was poured
To mark the youth a prophet of the Lord;
    And Jesse marveled, and his stalwart sons
      Stood mazed and wondering.

And from that hour the Spirit of the Lord
    Fell mightily on David, and he spoke
With wondrous wisdom, so that at his word
    The elders sought for counsel. And the folk,
      Beholding how his hand
Kept safe his father's sheep from prowling thief
And ravenous lion, made the lad the chief
    Of all their shepherds; so that David grew
      Illustrious in the land.

For all men praised him, and there went abroad
    A fame of him, as wise beyond his years
And strong and most courageous, one whom God
    Had highly honored, seeing that his ears
      Had heard the prophet's call;

A warrior with his weapons skilled to smite;
A minstrel who could strike the harp aright
    And sweetly sing. And so the rumor grew,
    And reached the ears of Saul.

II

For with the King it was as with a tree,
    O'ertopping all its fellows of the wood,
That spreads its boughs to heaven's immensity
    And drinks the stars and dew, and finds them good.

Beneath its shade the beasts lie down to rest,
    Among its leaves the song of birds is loud,
The wren and sparrow in its branches nest,
    The eagle stoops upon it from the cloud.

Then, through some rottenness, forgot of old,
    In branch or bark, the black wood-beetles bore,
And after them the fingers of the mould
    Creep, leprous white, and rot it to the core;

Yet still it flourishes and bears its fruit
    And lords it like a king among its kin,
While that pale death eats slow through trunk and root—
    Glad life without, but rottenness within;

And hears the cry go forth, "This tree so tall
    That towers to heaven, is rotten at the core.
Upon it let the woodmen's axes fall,
    And let its place behold it here no more!"

For that whereto the King had set his hand
    Had prospered: Moab, Zobah, Midian, all
Had sued for peace, and kings of far-off lands
    Sat restless on their thrones because of Saul.

DAVID

And he purveyed him purple robes from Tyre,
   And from Damascus brought a golden crown
Encrusted thick with gems like living fire,
   And lived in honor and in high renown.

But Samuel's sentence gnawed his vitals still,
   A leprous mould that struck through root and bough:
"The Lord hath sought a king to do His will;
   Thy neighbor, that is worthier than thou."

And Saul was troubled: though his hand had taken
   The spear and brand against the foes without
And drubbed them well, within, his soul was shaken
   By grisly ghosts of agony and doubt.

And even in his house the King went armed,
   With dagger hung at girdle, and a dart
Or javelin in his hand, the whiles he warmed
   The viper-eggs of murder in his heart.

The man that vexed him, brake his slightest law,
   Or came unbidden to his presence, took
His life in hand. Men drew their breath in awe,
   And all his household shunned his darkening look.

Then sleep forsook him, while he strained to catch
   Some doubtful sound of whispering at the doors,
And ghastly sighs, and fumblings at the latch,
   Or tread of furtive feet across the floors,

Where sound was none. Or if he slept, there came
   Such dreams as freeze the marrow: all the place
Would throng with monsters, shapes without a name,
   And bloated spiders crawled across his face;

And oftentimes he deemed himself hemmed round
   By fearful foemen, while the yielding sands
Gave way beneath his feet, and lo, he found
   His weapons turned to rushes in his hands.

Or, worst of all, a snake with human head
   And cloven tongue and scorpion tail, unrolled
From out the silken draperies of his bed,
   And coiled about his crown in scaly fold.

Then, wakening, he would weary to recall
   That semblance: Abner? Adriel?—one by one
He conned his household; captains, kinsmen, all
   He tested, but could fit the face to none.

And so, like smothering sands the hot winds heap
   About a desert spring, this horror grew,
And choked his manhood, waking or asleep,
   Till, false himself, he deemed all men untrue.

And those who knew him whispered that the Lord
   Had parted from him, and some dreadful guest—
A spirit from the nether world, abhorred
   And damned—had taken lodging in his breast.

Ahinoam the Queen, grown sick with care,
   Bedewed her couch with weeping night by night;
His daughters wept, his sons were in despair,
   And bearded captains groaned to see his plight.

For Saul would sit all day and gnaw his beard,
   And scarcely eat or drink, but pluck his vest
As if for vermin, while his glances veered
   From face to face, but never came to rest.

And then came rumors that their ancient foe
   Philistia stirred beside her shallow sea,
For some had heard her brazen trumpets blow
   And seen her chariots whirling o'er the lea.

And all men murmured, doubting in their mind,
   If once again that ever-threatening wave
Should rise, then whither should they turn to find
   (Saul being as he was) a man to save?

DAVID

>   Then Jonathan and Abner met, and spake
>   Of this new peril, saying, "We might lead
>   The host to battle—but if once they break
>   We cannot turn them, and are lost indeed."
>
>   And Abner said, "By God, I have a plan
>   To stir thy father from this depth of gloom,
>   But dread to wake the fury of the man—
>   As well to rouse a lion with a broom.
>
>   "The Philistines are mustering; this is plain.
>   And but for Saul I know of none to save.
>   Far better take his javelin through my brain
>   Than live, to be a filthy Cretan's slave."
>
>   The Prince agreed; the scheme was told to all
>   The household: Abner first should speak the word,
>   Then Adriel, in favor now with Saul,
>   Should second him. The rest, with one accord,
>
>   Should urge the same advice and keep it hot,
>   Divide his wrath amongst them as they could,
>   Until he yielded. Seldom was a plot
>   So laid against a ruler for his good.
>
>   They entered where the King, with tousled hair,
>   Sat hunched upon his throne; his javelin
>   Clutched hard in hand; his eyes, with venomous glare,
>   Smouldering in sockets of his shrunken skin.
>
>   And Abner spake at once, "O King, behold
>   The Lord hath sent a spirit to affright
>   My lord the King, to make his blood run cold
>   With fears by day and dreadful dreams by night.
>
>   "Command thy servants therefore that they find
>   A minstrel, skilled to play the harp and sing;
>   For harmony can soothe the troubled mind:
>   Let such an harper stand before the King,

DAVID

"And it shall be that when, by night or day,
   The terror or the vision break thy rest,
The man shall strike his harp and sing a lay
   To charm the evil spirit from thy breast."

Saul turned upon his uncle narrowing slits
   That seemed not human eyes. A snarling sound
Laid bare his teeth. He might have torn to bits
   A man that flinched; but Abner kept his ground,

And Adriel, cool as grapes in dew, replied,
   "Yea, let us have a minstrel. There is one
At Bethlehem; and not since Jubal died
   Could any play the harp like Jesse's son."

Then others took the word, and spake in praise
   Of David; named him comely, valiant, strong,
And wise of speech; no man could sing such lays
   Nor blend his harp so sweetly with the song.

And so they pressed him, till the peevish Saul,
   His listless fingers plucking at his sleeve,
His roving eyes yet searching floor and wall
   As if for spiders, gave them grudging leave.

Then Abner, knowing that the need was sharp,
   Sent messengers in haste, and bade them, "Bring
The son of Jesse here, to strike his harp
   And charm the evil spirit from the King."

And Jesse heard them speak in wonderment,
   Yet hasted to fulfill the King's command,
Laded an ass with bread and wine, and sent
   His present unto Saul by David's hand.

His brethren looked with envious eyes, and saw
   These preparations, while their hearts grew grim
With hidden wrath; but overborne by awe
   They held their peace, and dared not mock at him.

DAVID

III

For on such accidents—if there be aught
So fitly called in this vast universe
Where He is sovereign, whose majestic thought
Wields earth and ocean, and whose laws coerce
Sun, moon, and those wide wanderers of the height
That tramp the zodiac with hoofs of fire,
Who snared the Scorpion in His net of light,
Called forth by name Arcturus and the Lyre,
And brings the counsel of the wise to naught,
Lays low the proud, and thwarts the strong of their desire—

With things so slight—if anything be slight
In those long reaches of eternity
Where suns burn out like candles in the night,
And corals lift the islands from the sea—
Doth Destiny her works: the wanton's kiss,
The babblings of the fool; these topple down
The courts where Caesar and Semiramis
Ruled once in majesty, to set the crown
On serf or shepherd; and the strong man's might
Is brought to nothingness by one of no renown.

Yea so, this very terror of the King
Lest he should lose his kingdom, his concern
For safety of his crown, did madness bring
Upon him; and his madness made him turn
To David for release from his distress,
Lift up the lad to power, and then through shame
And hard injustice teach him kingliness,
That he might reign when Saul's own flickering flame
Was quenched in darkness; so that harp and sling
Go down the generations linked with David's name.

DAVID

For Jesse's son, bewildered by the call
From him he held for so much more than man
As scarcely less than God—and he so small
In Judah's thousands—took his harp, and ran,
Driving the ass before him, all that hard
And breathless journey, like a bird on wing,
To Gibeah. There the Captain of the Guard
Received the lad with kindly welcoming,
And sent him in; and David looked on Saul,
And all his hot blood sang, "The King! It is the King!"

There, too, he saw the Queen, and those fair maids
Her daughters: stately Merab, deep of breast,
Most like her mother with her dusky braids;
And slender Michal was the loveliest
Of lovely women, and her starry eyes,
Like those that charmed her father long ago,
Turned now on David in a soft surprise
And wonder, while her color mounted slow,
As when Astarte glimmers through the shades
Of twilight, rosy with a deepening afterglow.

And there was Adriel the Meholathite,
Betrothed of Merab, and young Phaltiel
Who sought the hand of Michal: men of might
And honor, who had served their master well
On many battlefields. But Jonathan
The Prince, and Abner, Captain of the Host,
Had left the court that very day, to scan
The threatening peril on Philistia's coast;
And merriment and mirth had taken flight,
For every cheek was pale, and Saul was like a ghost.

But David's entering was like a beam
Of sudden sunlight, in a house of gloom
From whose dark rafters tattered cobwebs stream,
When all the somber dust-motes of the room

DAVID

    Arise and shine; despairing glances drew
    And centered on the shepherd, as on one
    That bore the lamp of God; hope lived anew
    In Saul's dark brain; his thoughts began to run
    With lighter step; as one awaked from dream
    He looked upon the lad and loved him like a son.

    Strange meeting this! The King, whose soul was wasted
    By sins and follies, and the shepherd boy,
    His cup of manhood full but yet untasted:
    The gloom of madness, and the boundless joy
    Of budding life. And strange that love should spring
    Between the twain, though blighted soon by wrong
    And all those bitter envyings of the King,
    Yet held by David true his whole life long.
    And now, at signal from the King, he hasted
    To tune his shepherd's harp, and raised his voice in song:

    The evening hour is come; the sheep are folded,
        The shadows darken over sward and loam,
    The doves fly low, the ploughman and the shepherd
        Turn home, turn home.

    All day the sheep have wandered from their pastures,
        All day the plough hath turned the furrows long.
    How sweet is rest, when God gives rest from labor
        At evensong.

    Yea, pleasant are the milk, the bread and honey,
        To him that ploughs and him that keeps the sheep;
    And sweet to them the notes of pipe and zither;
        And sweet their sleep.

    God made the King the shepherd of His people;
        He sent the King to plough the fields of war.
    The King hath kept the sheep, and in the battle
        Was conqueror.

DAVID

He saved the flock of Israel from the slaughter;
   He furrowed Ammon with a share of steel;
He trod Philistia as the corn of threshing
   Beneath his heel.

And now the labors of the King are ended,
   The sheep are folded, and the furrows run.
Like homing birds the standards come from battle:
   The day is done.

Lord, give the King Thy rest, for he hath labored,
   And give the King Thy peace, and make him whole:
The burden of the day, the brunt of battle,
   Have bowed his soul.

Set forth for his delight the bread of beauty,
   The apples of desire, the wine and oil
Of strength and gladness; give him joy for ashes
   And rest for toil.

O Thou that givest the shepherd and the ploughman
   The kindly darkness when their labors cease,
Give also to the shepherd of Thy people
   Thy healing peace.

So sang the shepherd, while his harp kept pace
In chords now sweet as twittering birds, now loud
And shrill, or deepening to tumultuous bass,
As when the thunder rolls from cloud to cloud.
And they that listened felt the fire descend
Upon their hearts from God; an ecstasy
Ineffable. And when he made an end
And all stood rapt and silent, wonderingly
The King arose, with light upon his face,
And said, "The morn is come: the dreams are gone from me!"

And then he bade them bring him bread and wine,
And ate and drank; and there was solemn joy
Throughout the court, as when men see a sign

DAVID

    From Heaven. And all men praised the shepherd boy,
And shouted till the tumult shook the doors
And rafters, with such merriment as when
They bring the harvest to the threshing floors,
Or part the spoil among victorious men.
And Saul cried out, "The kingdom still is mine!
For God hath shown me grace, and I am whole again!"

    So day by day the son of Jesse played,
And sang the mighty deeds that Saul had done,
Of flashing spears, and brands on bucklers laid,
In battles fought beneath the desert sun.
And day by day the strength of Saul returned:
His cold blood kindled, hearkening to the tone
Of David's voice, until his spirit yearned
Once more to hear the battle-trumpets blown,
To have his limbs in glittering mail arrayed,
And feel his weapon shock on bronze and splintering bone.

    Saul gave the shepherd gifts; vowed he should bear
His shield in battle; had him taught to use
The spear, the brand, the buckler, how to care
For arms and armor, and how best to choose
Right weapons for his hand. But David's heart
Yearned for the Princess Michal, as the thorn
Yearns for the Spring; and he would mourn apart,
Believing she must hold his name in scorn,
The daughter of the King, so wondrous fair,
So far beyond the hopes of one but meanly born.

    And though within the breast of Michal, too,
The heart would stir and flutter like a bird
When David happened near her, and she grew
All warm and rosy if he spake a word,
She yet dissembled, as a damsel should;
Seemed cool as morning when her cheeks were hot,
And gay when she was sad; for maidenhood

Was ever thus, in palace or in cot.
Her thoughts might soar like swallows in the blue
When David plucked his harp; but David knew it not.

And so he pined and sickened, and would sing
Sometimes with wandering mind and faltering tongue;
And Saul, who marked him listless at the string,
Had ruth upon him, deeming him but young
And sick for home. And therefore when the word
From Abner came, that Gath was like a heap
Of swarming men at arms, and Gibeah heard
Saul's furious trumpets sounding from the steep,
Young Adriel bare the armor of the King,
And Saul sent David home to keep his father's sheep.

Goliath

I

Let harpings mingle with the trumpet's voice,
The crash of cymbal and the roll of drum
And melody of viol and of flute;
And let the daughters of the Philistines
Exult in all their cities, and rejoice
In dance and high procession: let them come
With sheaves of corn and clusters from the vines,
Scattering the golden grain and purple fruit
For votive offering at the sacred shrines.

Yea, come in naked virgin loveliness.
Let flowery garlands deck the milk-white bull
For sacrifice to Dagon of the Deep
Who guards our thousand galleys; to the bright
All-Mother Derketo, who bends to bless
The flock and field; and to the beautiful
And mighty Marna, herdman of the height,
Who drives the signs of heaven like golden sheep
Through azure fields, and girds himself in light.

For offerings are meet, with hymns of praise
And thankfulness, to them that sit on high,
From those on whom they have bestowed their joy
In measureless abundance! Sound the psalm,
Ye mortal maidens, walking earthly ways,

To bright immortals throned beyond the sky.
In gardens sweet with Asphodel and palm,
Who have the power to save or to destroy,
Yet dwell in radiant and unending calm.

O sing! But unto Dagon most of all
Let praise ascend—the god of wind and brine,
Surge-trampling sovereign of the furrowed foam,
Who bade wild Ocean's ever-heaving floors
Grow smooth before those splendid ships and tall
That bare Goliath, and its ripples shine
As quiet fish-pools, where the bending oars
Dipped flowing silver, while the sails drew home
The conqueror's galleys to his native shores.

In hour of need he comes; for he shall drive
The hosts of Israel as flocks of sheep,
And lead our armies to the victory
With shouts of triumph, while the trumpet peals
The cry of battle! Who shall hope to strive
With him whom strong immortals swear to keep?
Yea, he that shattered Sidon's oaken keels
And trod her strong-ribbed galleys in the sea,
Shall trample Israel beneath his heels.

II

Though confident, the Philistines began
The war with doubtful measures, as a man
Unsure of the event, will stand at guard
With weapon drawn, and view his foeman hard,
Hand, foot, and eye, and blade, as if in doubt
Lest he have matched his might with one too stout
To cope with; but at length he feigns a thrust,
Comes quick to parry, ready, if he must,
To ward a yet more vigorous return
Of the assault; for thus he hopes to learn

GOLIATH

The manly might of his antagonist,
His length of lunge, his suppleness of wrist,
The quickness of his eye—and so advance,
Retire or stand, according to the chance.
Not that they feared; for their diviners all
Agreed that neither Jonathan nor Saul
Could stand against their champion; and the Priest
Of Baalzebub at Ekron had released
A ghost from Hades, so that he was seen
Like smoke from burning seaweed, dimly green
Above the flame of sacrifice, to whom
He put the question: "Thou that from the tomb
Art come, give answer! For the fleshless dead
Are wiser than the living. Shall we tread
Our foemen underfoot, or shall we fall
Before the spears of Jonathan and Saul?"
The apparition wavered in the flame,
And harsh and ghastly hoarse an answer came,
Now plainly heard, now lost in choking sighs,
As when a wind blows fitfully and dies
In caves of sepulture; and they who heard
Avouched it for the very voice and word
Of Phicol, Lord of Ekron, him that died
Before Beth-aven, with his bannered pride.

  "The fiat stands forever:
   All things begun have ending.
  What Fate ordains, endeavor
   Hath not the hope of mending.
  The dead are but beholders,
   The future half discerning;
  Yet know the fire that smoulders
   May burst to fiercest burning.

  "Your champion shall be never
   By foeman's sword brought under:
  None but his own can sever
   His flesh and soul asunder.

GOLIATH

    The deathless gods have fenced him:
    Till earth herself assail him
    And stone rise up against him
    His might shall never fail him."

Here blent the voice with sighs and stifled groans
Of such an anguish that the listeners' bones
Were frozen to the marrow; yet the sound
Went mumbling on, like water underground,
Now heard, now lost. No ordered speech it seemed,
But bits of broken thought, like something dreamed
And half recalled on waking, while the flame
Burned sputtering on the altar. Then it came
Once more with clearness:

                  "Neither shall your might
Be broken, nor your armies put to flight,
Till Israel's anointed King shall wear
A shepherd's cloak and locks of ruddy hair."

With such auspicious oracle to cheer
Their hearts, Philistia's nobles felt no fear;
Yet Achish counseled them—and all the rest,
Who knew him wise, agreed the plan was best—
To feign a weak attack, assail some near
And feeble territory, as in fear
Of venturing much, with but a slender band;
And these should ravage and lay waste the land
Till Saul came forth to battle; then engage
His force in combat, and arouse his rage
With semblance of resistance, till they found
Their band outnumbered; then to yield their ground
Perforce and with reluctance; so in hopes
Of easy triumph Saul might leave the slopes
Of Israel's rugged mountains, his defense
In other wars, with foolish confidence
Of victory, and carry the campaign
Upon Philistia's flat and open plain,

GOLIATH

Where they might cut him off, and plough his force
With rushing chariot and iron-shod horse.

Though Achish counseled wisely, his designs
Were less for safety of the Philistines
Than for his own. A wolf with teeth too blunt
To tussle with the dogs, whene'er the hunt
Pressed close, as oft it did—for kings who hold
Their thrones by craft, o'er warlike men and bold,
Do seldom win their love—he did not fail
Of guile to double and confuse his trail,
Or lead the pack into a hornet's hive
Or match them with a bear, and so contrive
To get them stung or mauled. And, having dealt
In many a cunning trick to save his pelt
He wore it still. But now he needed all
His strategy. Scant fear he had of Saul,
Since rumor said the man was going mad
And kept his house; but Achish knew he had
A rival in Goliath for his throne,
A foe implacable. He long had known
That he must reckon with the blond-haired giant,
Who, lawless in his youth and half defiant
Of Achish, as he grew in strength and years,
And learnt to splinter skulls and laugh at spears,
Had gained a following of the wild and young
Among his people—witless fools that hung
Upon his witless jests, and made him vain
As well as lawless, swearing he might reign
Far better than the King. And though he heard
All this and more, King Achish spake no word
Of censure, but assumed to be his friend
While working for his ruin. In the end
He called the giant in and feasted him
With food and flattery, praised his strength of limb,

His courage and his prowess; offered ships
And gold, and urged the fellow to eclipse
The power of Sidon, vowing he should sweep
Phoenicia's hard-beaked galleys from the deep,
And make Philistia mistress of the brine.

Goliath, filled with compliments and wine,
Consented, and the rest was quickly done:
Still brimmed with drink, he sailed from Ashkelon
With all his mad companions, while a score
Of galleys churned the foam with keel and oar;
A splendid fleet, of which he seemed to be
High Admiral. Around him rang the sea
With cheers and laughter. Then the giant slept,
And all his fellows, while a hard wind swept
Their galley seaward. When the stinging brine
That leaped the bulwarks cleared his wits of wine,
He looked upon a sea that had no shore,
Unwhitened by a sail, undipped by oar.
Beneath him rolled a galley, ill-equipped,
And wallowing gunwales-under as she shipped
The brine by bucketfuls; a shark's fin clave
The sea; the loud wind shouted to the wave.

And in his lordly palace, Achish, grim
Yet smiling, prayed the deep might swallow him.

The end was otherwise. They fought the sea
And conquered, though the waves incessantly
Washed over them, and though the galley drank
The sea, through worm-holes in her rotting plank;
They bailed and caulked, and cursed the King of Gath
And all his works, in bitterness and wrath,
And prayed for vengeance, while the sun declined
Before them, and the darkness came behind
And covered them with terrors. With the dawn
Came freshening hope, and still they labored on,

GOLIATH

And in the end their ship rode high and dry
On sunshot waves; yet they were like to die
From thirst and hunger.

      But they chanced to meet,
The second dawn thereafter, with a fleet
Sailing from Africa, with store of gold
And sandalwood and ivory in hold,
And heavy with their cargoes. Part by dint
Of swift assault, but mainly from the glint
Of level sun in the Phoenician's eyes,
They dashed among them, took them by surprise,
Rammed two and swamped them, grappled with a third
And smashed her oars. Then Sidon's seamen heard
Goliath's war-shout, thunderous and deep
As surf on shingle; saw the giant leap
Like Ares on their bulwark, and the rest
Came leaping after, grappling breast to breast
With the Sidonians. Taken unaware,
The shipmen fought in fury and despair,
Dashed down upon their deck, or tossed like swine
To feed the shark or strangle in the brine.

The other galleys, crowding oar and sail,
Escaped to Sidon, where they told their tale—
How sea-born monsters, slavering foam and blood,
Had dragged their comrades quick beneath the flood,
And crushed their ships like eggs.

       The Philistines
Grudged not their going: here was store of wines
And food and treasures, and beneath their feet
A sturdy galley, stout enough to beat
Through any storm. The larger of the twain
They rammed could be repaired, to ride again
Upon the seas; nor did their captives fail
Sufficient mariners to handle sail

And man the oars. And though they saw the ship
They late had quitted, with her seams a-rip
From figurehead to rudder, from the shock
Of war, heel over, plunging like a rock
Beneath the sea, the gods had served them well,
Who gave two galleys for a rotten shell
And boundless plenty for their pinching dearth.
Goliath bellowed with colossal mirth,
Beholding while the worm-bit galley sank,
And cried, "O Achish, we have cause to thank
The gods and thee! May mighty Marna bless
Thy noble house, and Dagon give success
Like this to every deed of thine, till we
Return and pay thee for thy courtesy!"

Thereafter years had passed. Goliath sailed
The seas, while Sidon, Tyre, and Hippo wailed
For galleys captured, cargoes made a spoil,
And seamen flung to sharks, or forced to toil
At alien oarlocks; and they combed the seas
From Ilium to the Gates of Hercules,
From Africa to Europe, while they laid
Such treasures on his head as would have paid
The ransom of a king. Their navies churned
The seas with fruitless questings, and returned
Without their prey; or, evil-starred, they found
The fair-haired corsair, and their ships were ground
Beneath his plunging keels. Wild rumor told
What treasures he had gathered—bars of gold
From Ophir, silver, emeralds, ivory,
And scarlet wool: on all that went by sea
He levied tribute. But the ships that bare
Philistia's ensigns traveled everywhere
In safety; for the giant loved the land
That gave him birth, and would not lift a hand
Against her peace.

GOLIATH

       And now, obedient
To summons by Philistia's Council sent,
He had returned. His ships, with silent oars
And folded sails, were hauled upon the shores
At Ashkelon. Once more Goliath trod
His native soil; and all but as a god
Men did him honor: street and temple rang
The praises of his deeds, while damsels sang
Before him, scattering garlands wreathed of bloom,
And hailing him the Scourge of Tyre, the Doom
Of Sidon's ships, the mighty one, whose hand
Should bring deliverance to Philistia's Land.

As yet he tarried near his ships, the guest
Of Hanun; but to Achish had addressed
A message, framed in words of courteous speech,
Like messengers that bow the knee, yet each
A dagger fingers in its velvet sheath—
So seemed the message fair, but underneath
Were mockery and vengeance and disdain:
"Goliath, trampler of the boundless main,
To Achish, Sovereign King of Gath: My Lord
Thy servant hath returned, and doth accord
To thee all reverence; for yet he hath
Remembrance how, when he abode at Gath,
Thou didst him kindness, which he would requite
With full, unstinted guerdon in the sight
Of mortals and of gods. But first of all
Thy servant hath an ambassage to Saul,
Philistia's Council having bade him go.
When he hath rid his country of her foe,
Goliath will return to Gath, and bring
With his own hand his blessing to the King.
His gifts to thee are sword and spear and helm:
And he will pledge his head to purge thy realm
Of men who practice treachery in guise
Of hospitality; who tell their lies

GOLIATH

To men bemused with wine; and all who send
A man to death, while claiming him for friend,
Or hide their dirks in garlands; though they dwell
In thine own house. Until that hour, farewell."

Here lay the gage of war. The words, though fair,
To Achish' eyes were glittering swords, made bare
For slaughter. If the giant vanquished Saul
And came in triumph, naught could stay the fall
Of Achish and his house. The other lords
Would lift no hand to aid him; and the swords
That girt him round, his chariots, his bright
Array of spears— What were they to the might
Of this one man, whose naked hand could crush
A bullock's skull as if it brake a rush?
He saw his ruin: all his schemes had gone
Awry, and smiling Destiny had drawn
His thread and snapped it. Fate but mocked at him:
He saw himself dismembered, limb from limb
Torn off, as children pluck a cricket's legs
To see its agony. His peacock's eggs
Were hatching basilisks. He felt his end
Upon him: Time was left his only friend.
Though weak in battle, he was reckoned wise
In war by all, and what he should advise
The lords would hearken to. Though fierce and rude,
Goliath would not press a private feud
In time of war; and he must find a way
To lengthen out the conflict, and delay
The day of reckoning.

                His anguished mind
Went questing to and fro, yet could not find
An exit from the trap: escape was none.
So might a captive leopard, one by one
Survey the bars that hedge his narrow den,
From end to end, and then begin again

GOLIATH

            His hopeless circuit. Then his thought laid hold
On Atarah the Sorceress: she had told
The truth, the cursèd truth; and he had braved
The other lords' displeasure, and had saved
Her life from their vindictive hate, with thought
That she might serve him yet. And now he sought
The hold where she was prisoned.

                                    From the bloom
Of grove and garden to that place of doom
Was but a step: so nigh to earth is Hell
With all its torments. In the stifling cell
He gasped for breath. The cresset's ruddy glare
Revealed a scene of woe to raise the hair
And freeze the marrow. Shackled hand and heel
To that rough stone that ground the barley meal,
And blinking at the sudden light with eyes
Where misery had blotted out surprise,
Was Atarah; and Achish' crooked smile
Played over her. No need was here of guile:
The hag would do his bidding, as the damned
Obey the Prince of Devils. Achish jammed
The door ajar for air. "Our fables say
The mouse hath helped the lion in his day.
I saved thee once from death: be thou the mouse
To cut my snare, and from the prison house
Thou shalt go free." A sound of twittering birds
And whispering water mingled with his words
Like sounds from Paradise, and through the stink
There crept a scent of myrtle leaves that drink
The sun all day. Her hopeless eyes accused
The king in silence, while her tongue, unused
To speech, moved soundlessly; her lips, at first
Dry like the lips of them that die with thirst
Or burn with fever, found at last a hoarse,
Unearthly utterance, fit for intercourse

With shades from Erebus. "Enough," said she,
"That Hell and all its demons mock at me.
Must thou mock too?" He said, "I do not mock.
The Titan shackled to the Scythian rock
Was happier than thou: he had the sun
And all the free, wide heaven to look upon,
Though Marna he defied. But in the end
He yielded to the god, and made him friend.
Be taught of him. The power is in my hand
To make thee free." She said, "Though I should stand
Where Moses stood on Nebo, with the earth
Stretched wide before, my eyes could see but dearth
And desert, and the broad estates of Hell
Consumed with fire. I doomed myself to dwell
In Tartarus: my soul is its own place
Of torment and despair, because the Face
Of God is turned away. I sinned the sin
Of sorcery. Thou canst neither shut me in
Nor set me free."

    Then something like to ruth
Shook Achish' throat; for he had seen her youth
With all its starry beauty. Could this hag,
Gray, wrinkled, vile, with but a filthy rag
For covering, be Atarah, who taught
The heart of Saul to leap, and after wrought
His madness by her loss? Could beauty turn
To dust? He questioned, "Is thy God more stern
Than mortal man? Behold, I pity thee,
Who hate thy people. How much more shall He
Whom thou adorest? Lo, I too have sinned,
And retribution rides on every wind.
Hope thou for mercy from thy God, and show
Like mercy unto me." She said, "I know
Thy thought, O Achish; for of old I wooed
Thy gods as lovers, and my soul imbrued

GOLIATH

    In magic lore, rejoicing that my spell
Could call reluctant demons out of Hell
And make them answer. Now they come unsought,
And vex my soul with revelations brought
To ears unwilling. Though for no reward
Will I pursue again that trade abhorred,
Yet since thou savedst my life—though to what end
I do not know—I now will be thy friend,
And tell to thee the vision that I saw
When thou didst last command me to withdraw
The veil that hides the future. In my trance
I saw thy hosts and Israel's advance
And clash in battle. Then a burly giant
Came forth from out thy host, and stood defiant
Between the camps, and challenged Israel's host
For one to fight him to the uttermost.
The rest was dim, confused, and dark with doubt
And shadow; but meseemed that Saul went out
To give him battle, and the giant's blade
Heaved high to smite the King. But when I prayed
To Israel's God the vision changed: there came
A shepherd boy, with hair like ruddy flame,
Who bare no sword or shield, but slang a stone
That crushed the giant's casque and cracked the bone
And laid him flat; then drew the giant's sword
And clave his mighty neck; and so he poured
His blood upon the ground: whereon I praised
The Living God."

                King Achish stood amazed
A little space, then spake: "This serveth well
For commentary on the oracle
Of Ekron, which declared the giant's life
Secure, till stone should stand with him in strife
And his own steel should slay him—words that leave
The mind persuaded; but I now perceive

GOLIATH

They hold a double meaning. Paradox
As yet remains: this keeper of the flocks
Should be a king, if there indeed be aught
Of truth in oracles: But thou hast bought
Thy pardon with thy vision. Thou art free
Of all my realm, and I will give to thee
Thy daily portion. Thou shalt have a room
That opens on a garden sweet with bloom
And summer fruits." She asked, "Hast thou a key
To loose me from my guilt, or set me free
From mine own soul? Where'er the body dwell,
The soul estranged from God abides in Hell."
Thereon she bowed her head upon the stone
And spake no more. And Achish, with a groan,
Stole forth into the garden, with the cool
Of evening shadows over sward and pool,
And there he made his plans.

                              There might be truth
Hid somehow in that oracle uncouth
By Phicol uttered—if 'twere he who spoke
From that green shadow in the altar-smoke—
And that the witch had looked behind the veil
He did not doubt, nor that she told her tale
With honesty. And yet, to trust too much
In oracle or vision were to clutch
At straws in flood. If shepherd-boy or king
Should slay Goliath with a stone and sling,
Then all were well. If not, himself must win
The victory over Saul to save his skin—
Gain honor with the nobles and the throng,
And leave his foe no laurels. He was strong
In chariots: he must order the campaign
To draw the enemy upon the plain,
And win renown, if it were possible,
By slaying Saul. And if Goliath fell

GOLIATH

    Before some charioteer who drave amiss
In rush of battle, who should see in this
Aught save the chance of war? And Time remained
His friend: each added day of warfare gained
Were one day more of life.

                            The lords gave heed
To his device, discussed it, and agreed.
And Achish ranked his chariots between
Ashdod and Timnath, in the level green
Of meadow-lands, where they had space to run
In furious course. The Lord of Ashkelon,
The fierce and fiery Hanun, led a band
Of twenty thousand spears against the land
Of western Judah, and began to sweep
The pastures bare of cattle and of sheep
And slay the helpless folk; but soon was stayed
From pillaging, when Saul came forth, arrayed
For battle. Then there followed petty fights
Of roving band with band, among the heights
And wild ravines; but still did not the two
Main hosts encounter, for the foe withdrew
Toward Ashdod and the sea, as they had planned,
To lure King Saul upon the level land
Where lay their chariot-force. But Saul, aware
Of peril in the lowlands, shunned the snare,
Retreating in his turn; and Hanun wheeled
And followed after, while his trumpets pealed
Their shrill defiance. Then King Saul essayed
To trap the Philistines; for, having made
Division of his host, he gave one corps
To Abner, bidding him retreat before
The enemy, while he, in circuit wide,
Encompassed Hanun's force, and occupied
The road to Gath. But Hanun, who had learned
The wiles of Saul in other wars, discerned

GOLIATH

The stratagem, and leading back his legion
Encamped upon a hillside, in the region
Of Socoh and Azekah; and the force
Of Israel pitched beside a water-course
In Elah's Vale. Here either host could view
The other's camp, and neither would renew
The conflict. So a while the war stood still:
Saul kept the vale and Hanun held the hill,
And neither one advantage could obtain.
Saul would not be enticed upon the plain,
Nor Hanun suffer Saul to bar the way
Of his retreat.

              At last, upon a day,
Goliath sought the Lord of Ashkelon:
"By Dagon's head," he asked, "shall Summer run
Her lazy course, while on the harbor beach
My ships lie warping and their ensigns bleach,
And we, like children, play at hunt the hare?
Give me thy leave to send a challenge fair
To Saul for single combat, that the war
Be settled by the issue. I abhor
This idleness."

              Then Hanun gave him leave,
And he arrayed himself with helm and greave
And shirt of mail, and he that bare his shield
Went on before. The champion stood revealed
Between the camps, and shouted forth his cry
To Israel's army, saying, "I defy
The host of Israel. Are not ye the swine
Of Saul? And am I not a Philistine?
Let Saul come forth to me; or if he fears,
Then let him choose the mightiest of his spears
To do me battle. Then if I shall slay
Your champion, all Israel shall obey

GOLIATH

The Philistines and serve them; but if he
Shall vanquish me and slay me, then shall ye
Be masters over us. By all the high
Immortals whom we worship, I defy
Your King, your gods, and you." Then stood he still,
So huge he seemed a hill upon a hill,
While Israel looked upon him, marveling
That from the loins of Noah there should spring
A man so big, or if, from years of old,
That giant race survived, of whom was told
That they were gendered when those renegades
From realms celestial wedded mortal maids,
Before the deluge. And a shudder passed
Through all the army: Abner stood aghast,
And Saul, who ne'er had blenched before the face
Of mortal man, stood trembling in his place
And could not speak.

      The Philistine perceived
Their consternation, and his shoulders heaved
With Titan laughter. Such a roar of mirth,
To shake the sky and terrify the earth,
The Cyclops might have vented, when he found
Ulysses' seamen sleeping on the ground
That floored his cavern. Mountain answering hill,
That monstrous laugh went rolling onward still,
Flung back from cliff and woodland, peal on peal,
While the colossus turned upon his heel
And sought his tent.

      Thereafter, day by day
At point of noon, in glittering array,
Goliath, standing in the selfsame place,
Reproached the host of Israel to the face,
Blasphemed their God, and mocked their King who saw
His enemy in arms, and durst not draw

His sword against him. And though Saul decreed
That he would give his daughter for the meed
Of him that slew the giant, and that he
And all his house henceforward should be free
From tax and tribute, there was none to dare
Such certain death, for even a prize so fair.

III

But in the fields of Bethlehem
   Young David kept the sheep.
He pastured them on grasses green
In meadows fragrant and serene;
In heat of noon he guided them
   By waters still and deep.

They trusted in his staff and rod;
   He knew his sheep by name—
Pomegranate-blossom, Apple, Rose,
Snow-fleece and Lily, Ruby-nose,
Dawn-star and Cloud and Lentil-pod—
   He called them, and they came.

At dawn, across the dewy wold,
   He led them forth afar;
He drave the prowling wolf away,
Nor let the bear and lion slay,
And brought them back to friendly fold
   Beneath the evening star.

It should be filled with joyous things,
   The life a shepherd leads;
To roam the windy hilltops high
Where fleecy clouds go drifting by,
To hear the wild bird when it sings,
   And blow his pipe of reeds.

GOLIATH

> But David's heart was lone and sad,
>   And David's soul was sore,
> For Michal, daughter of the King,
> The starry-eyed, the ravishing;
> And this was all the thought he had:
>   "I shall not see her more."
>
> Each morning came the thought of her,
>   A wonder blent with pain.
> And as he led his flocks away,
> Her eyes would glimmer through the gray
> Of morning shadows, lovelier
>   Than roses after rain.
>
> And morn, and noon, and evening,
>   His mind this burden bore,
> Repeated like the snatch of song
> A foolish bird sings all day long:
> "She is the daughter of the King:
>   I shall not see her more."
>
> A woeful song the lad would sing
>   Her gentleness to praise:
> How she was beautiful and wise,
> And soft of speech and fair of eyes.
> The little lambs stood listening;
>   The sheep forgot to graze.
>
> Oh fair is she, the daughter of the King,
>   And none is like to her.
> The doves that cleave the air on snowy wing
> Are wondrous fair, and all the blooms of Spring,
> The flowers of God that know no withering;
>   But she is lovelier.

Her eyes are radiant as the stars that light
   Dim pastures with their beams.
Her words are birds of gold that sing in flight
Through Eden's Garden; flutes that play by night
Unseen; and all her thoughts are lilies white
   That bloom by whispering streams.

A fragrant myrtle tree is she, that grows
   On lofty Lebanon;
A fountain in a desert place; a rose
Among the thorns; a meadow hid by snows;
A watered garden; yea, a wind that blows
   From hills of cinnamon.

Yea, fair is she, the daughter of the King,
   Beyond all maids that are.
What offering may a simple shepherd bring
To her who hath all loveliness—the Spring,
The dew of morning and the bird a-wing,
   Dawn-light and evening star?

He brought her love: what other gift had he?
   Red coral, golden ring,
The twisted shells yet singing of the sea,
Or silken veil, or silvery filigree—
No gift had I but love to bring to thee,
   O daughter of the King.

O fair art thou and radiant art thou,
   Bright star of morning sky,
Whom gentleness and loveliness endow
With wondrous gifts! Lo, God hath set thee now
A golden apple on a silver bough,
   For mortal hopes too high!

GOLIATH

    Yet let me still rejoice that I have seen,
      O daughter of the King,
    Thy beauty in its bloom; that I might lean
    An hour beside thee; as old men who glean
    Through sunburnt fields remember meadows green
      Set thick with buds of Spring.

    The song was done; but David's hand
      Yet lingered on the lyre
    And called its notes forth one by one,
    As when the light of day is done
    The afterglow still floods the land
      With slowly fading fire.

    The music died on muted strings,
      And stillness fell on all
    The pastures, save that from the thorn
    A cricket wound his elfin horn;
    A beetle passed on droning wings;
      A cuckoo's far-off call

    Came faintly from a cedar's top;
      A partridge whistled shrill
    Among the stubble; and the sheep,
    Like wisps of cloud awaked from sleep,
    Stirred softly, and began to crop
      The grasses of the hill.

    Now Jesse's elder sons had gone
      To battle with King Saul.
    Strong warriors they, and fierce and hard;
    Eliab, russet-bearded, scarred,
    Abinidab with iron brawn,
      And Shimeah, brown and tall.

And days had flown, and Jesse's heart
  Was troubled over them.
No word of how the battle fared,
Nor what they did, nor what they dared,
Nor if they bravely did their part,
  Had come to Bethlehem.

And so he called his shepherd-son,
  The lad with ruddy hair,
And bade him, "Go, to-morrow morn,
And take thy brethren roasted corn
And cheese and bread; then hither run
  And tell me how they fare."

And David rose at break of day,
  When yet the sky was pale,
And while a servant kept the sheep,
By field and wold and slope and steep,
He hastened blithely all the way,
  And came to Elah's Vale.

Two hillocks from the valley rose,
  And on the one was seen
The camp of Saul, with parapet
And bank and stakes in order set,
While on the other pitched their foes,
  Beyond a deep ravine.

The armies stood for war arrayed,
  And fair their ensigns flew,
But all was like a stale at chess:
The ordered ranks stood motionless,
And not a warrior drew his blade
  And not a trumpet blew.

GOLIATH

IV

Who hath not heard the tale? And who that breathes
Can hear of David's deed, nor feel his blood
Run hot and high, like Ocean when it seethes
Round rocky headlands, while its waves in flood
Leap roaring at the sky, and foaming scud
Drives white before the wind? For Time bequeaths
No laurels with a luster like to this,
Though gathered on the sounding shores of Troy;
Nor hath Thermopylae or Salamis
Or rugged Rome a splendor such as wreathes,
To earth's last hour, the head of Judah's shepherd boy.

He stood among his brethren at the line
Of outer ramparts, while the sun rode high
In midmost heaven, and saw the Philistine
Stride forth from his pavilion to defy
The host of Israel. Of Tyrian dye
His tunic was; and like a porcupine
He bristled from his helmet to his shoon
In mail. His buckler seemed a chariot-wheel,
His spear a galley's mast; and like the noon
He burned upon the hillside, all one shine
Of gold and blinding brass and bronze and burnished steel.

So striding to his place, he opened wide
The beaver of his helmet, with a crash
Brought down his spear-butt on the earth, and cried,
"Get back to kennel ere ye feel the lash,
Ye dogs of Israel! Wherefore will ye gnash
Your teeth at freeborn men? I have defied
Your King and God, and held you up to scorn
These forty days, and still ye show no sign
Of manhood. Are ye, then, of women born,
Or whelped by jackals, that ye will not bide
To stand with sword and shield against a Philistine?"

Then David asked the soldiers who stood nigh,
"What godless man is this, and insolent,
Who dares reproach Jehovah, and defy
The host of Israel? Shall the braggart vent
His scorn upon the King, and none be sent
To give him answer, prove his boast a lie?
For God can give a stripling strength to smite
This Philistine. Though he be fierce and fell
And filled with boasting, in Jehovah's sight
He yet is nothing. And the man should die
Who scorns our King and mocks the Rock of Israel!"

Thereat Eliab gave him answer rude,
And called him fool, and bade him hold his tongue.
But others, who beheld the lad imbued
With valor and discretion, though so young,
And now to fiery indignation stung,
Replied that whosoever took this feud
Against the giant, by the King's decree,
If he should slay Goliath in the strife,
His father's house from tribute should be free,
And he with princely honors be endued,
And have the daughter of the King to be his wife.

Then some forewarned him of the monster's might
And prowess. He had slain a thousand men
With naked hands, they said, nor feared to fight
The many-headed hydra in his den
Or yoke the Colchian oxen. Yea, and when
He feasted after battle, he would bite
The flesh from living captives, crunching bones
With bear-like tushes, whiles he wrenched apart
The hip and shoulder, laughing at their groans
And curses, reveling in foul delight
To stuff his mighty maw with liver, lungs, and heart.

GOLIATH

Then Abner, passing by and marking how
Their words had kindled David, till his face
Was crimson to the temples, and his brow
Grown dark with wrath for Israel's disgrace,
He took the lad, and led him to the place
Where Saul lay sick; for once again his mind
Was overcome with fears: his eyes burned hot
With fever, and he listlessly reclined
Upon his couch, half mad. And looking now
Upon the shepherd lad, it seemed he knew him not.

And David cried, "Let no man's spirit fail,
O King, because this giant hath defied
Our host. Although he gird himself with mail
And be so big, the Lord is on our side;
And He will humble him, and dash his pride
Headlong in dust. Thy servant will assail
This haughty Philistine, and thou shalt see
How swift destruction comes on him who boasts
Against the Lord. Behold, his sword shall be
As nothing; neither shall his spear prevail
On him who sets his trust upon the God of Hosts."

Then Saul was moved, and said, "Thou canst not wage
Such war as this; for thou art but a youth,
And he a man of war from earliest age."
But David said, "My Lord, I tell thee truth:
The Lord who saved me from the lion's tooth
And from the bear, that robbed my heritage,
Will save me also on the battlefield.
He will deliver me, and overthrow
This mighty Philistine, despite his shield
And harness. Wherefore should I dread his rage?
He is but flesh and blood, and God can lay him low."

Thereon the King commanded them to brace
His armor on the lad, and let him go,
For God had sent him. Then did Adriel lace
The gorget, dinted deep with many a blow
Of brand and spear; the helmet settled low
Upon his head, and hid the boyish face.
They trussed him in the cuirass, bound the greave
On either leg, and made him prisoner
In jingling mail. But when he sought to leave
The tent, he stood as rooted in his place,
Borne down by such a weight of arms he could not stir

Then Adriel smote his thigh, and filled the air
With sudden mirth, as from the hollow casque
There came a mournful voice: "I cannot bear
This iron burden. It would overtask
A camel's strength. My Lords, I did not ask
For kingly armor: only let me wear
My shepherd's linen shirt, and take my sling,
With five smooth pebbles, such as shepherds throw
At dogs, and I will make his helmet sing
Around his ears; and if I hit him fair
Between the eyes, he will not need a second blow."

So Adriel took the helmet from his head,
And stripped the harness off him, and he shook
His ruddy locks and laughed. And Abner said,
"God be thy strength, young man." Then David took
Five shining pebbles chosen from the brook,
And four were white as milk, and one was red,
With veins of azure: just the weight and size
He best could use. But Saul could not confine
His grief, and water stood in Adriel's eyes,
As David, swordless and unhelmeted,
With staff in hand went forth to fight the Philistine.

GOLIATH

The shepherd stood between the camps, and cried,
"Come forth, Goliath, if thou dare to meet
A man of Israel! God hath seen thy pride,
And summons thee to His Imperial Seat
To hear thy doom. The fowls of heaven shall eat
Thy carcase, seeing that thou hast defied
The Lord of Hosts." Whereon the giant came,
And seeing but a stripling with a stave
He boiled with wrath, and cursed him in the name
Of all his gods, and said, "May Hell fly wide
And crush thee flat between her crooked teeth, thou slave!"

Then David hasted, and the giant rushed
To meet him, though encumbered by his mail
On that rough ground, his arms that might have crushed
Behemoth, swinging like a thresher's flail;
And Israel's warriors uttered one long wail,
Beholding David's blood before it gushed,
His body rent in pieces ere he fell,
And hearing even now his death-cry blend
With crack of bones and that derisive yell
Of triumph from Philistia—then stood hushed
With pity and despair, and waited for the end.

But David ran; and as he ran he slang
His stone—the red one with the veins of blue—
With all his strength. And deep and low it sang,
A song that rose to shrillness as it flew
With gathering speed. It lighted fair and true
Upon Goliath's helmet, with a bang
Like sledge on anvil; to the Philistine
No stroke of hammer, but the deafening roar
Of Doomsday's trumpet. Like an axe-bit pine
He tottered, and fell headlong with a clang
That shook the earth; and there he lay, and moved no more.

GOLIATH

And David came, and drew the giant's blade
From out its scabbard, and he set his heel
Upon his breast, and with the sword he made
A shining circle like a silver wheel
About his head, and so he drave the steel
Through that tough neck and slew him. Then he laid
The glaive across his shoulders, and returned
To Israel's camp. But there was mighty wrath
Among the Philistines when they discerned
Their champion dead. And Saul his host arrayed
And smote the Philistines unto the gates of Gath.

Adullam

I

Now when Saul returned victorious from the war
    in Elah's Vale,
  From the sack of Hanun's baggage and the
      ruin of his host,
  He had left the road to Ekron strewn with men
      and shattered mail,
    Like the heaps of shell and seaweed on a
      tempest-trodden coast.

  He had ravined like a lion at the very gates of
      Gath,
    With the smoke of burning vineyards he had
      blistered Ekron's eyes,
  And the mighty of Philistia he had slaughtered
      in his wrath;
    He had brought their spoil for booty, and their
      treasures for his prize.

  And the shepherd lad he honored, knowing
      praises were his due
    Who had slain the great Goliath with a pebble
      and a sling:
  He had put a ring upon him and a robe of
      purple hue,
    And had set him o'er the weapons and the
      armor of the King.

ADULLAM

Though the youth was puffed with triumph, yet
    he blamed him not for that—
  Little wonder, with the clamor all the host of
    Israel made!
He had put his life in peril, and had laid the
    giant flat,
  When the princes and the captains had not
    dared to gird a blade.

Nor had Jonathan displeased him, when he gave
    the lad his bow
  And his quiver and apparel, yea, his girdle
    and his sword,
Pledging deathless love—though David had but
    struck a single blow,
  For the man had mocked Jehovah, and the
    thing was of the Lord.

But when women came rejoicing all through
    countryside and town,
  With their castanets and timbrels, chanting
    the victorious strain,
And the matrons sang in dances, "Saul hath hewn
    his thousands down,"
  And the damsels answered, "David hath his tens
    of thousands slain!"

Then the King was filled with envy, and
    embittered were his days;
  Dagger-keen, the insult pierced him to the
    marrow of the bone.
"When the women thus misprize me, giving
    David higher praise,
  What is left the men to give him but the
    kingdom and the throne?"

ADULLAM

    So he eyed the lad thenceforward with a sick
        and crafty fear,
      Sent him oft on dangerous errands, hoping
        that he might be slain;
    But the Lord who rules the battle shielded him
        from sword and spear:
      Cherubim, encamped around him, brought
        him safely home again.

    Then Saul's servants told him, saying, "Lo, thy
        daughter, Michal fair,
      Sets her heart in love on David." And he laid
        a subtil plan:
    "He shall wed her to his ruin. Let the damsel be
        a snare.
      As they take a bear with honey, set a maid to
        catch a man."

    Then he bade them speak with David, tell him,
        "Lo, the people love thee,
      And the King in thee delighteth. Be thou
        strong and undismayed:
    Bring an hundred heads of warriors from the
        Philistines, to prove thee
      Worthy of the King's alliance: thou shalt wed
        the royal maid."

    "For," said Saul, "the youth is noble, and a shame
        it were to bind him
      And to hang him like a robber, for indeed
        he served me well.
    Let Philistia be against him; let the hand of
        Hanun find him.
      Let him perish like a warrior where the shouts
        of battle swell."

ADULLAM

And when David heard the message, all his
    heart was filled with singing
  As a thicket sings in April when the birds are
    in the trees:
"Lovely Michal! I would win thee, though the
    price of thee were bringing
  All the lions of the desert and the dragons of
    the seas!"

Then he led his band of sworders down against
    the Philistines,
  In the season of the vintage, when the folk
    were reveling;
Slew two hundred lusty fellows, while they
    danced among the vines,
  And he brought their heads to Gibeah, and he
    gave them to the King.

But the King his spleen dissembled, as a ruffian
    cloaks his sword
  (Naught avail the hunter's meshes if the lion
    have been roused),
Ordered sheep and oxen slaughtered, zithers
    played, and flagons poured,
  And he called his friends and kinsmen to
    behold the pair espoused.

Merry was the day of marriage; sweetly did the
    minstrels play,
  Champions leaped and raced and wrestled,
    shot the bow and cast the pike,
And the King was loud in laughter, seeming
    gayest of the gay—
  So a bravo hides his dagger, waiting for the
    chance to strike.

ADULLAM

    And he blessed them both, and kissed them,
        saying to his daughter, "Be
      Fruitful, and thy children plenteous as the
        sheaves the reaper gathers!
    Thou mayest bear a son to David who shall reign
        in place of me,
      That my kingdom be not broken when I sleep
        among my fathers."

    David answered, "God forbid it! Long and
        glorious be thy reign,
      And let Jonathan succeed thee. Let the tribes
        of men adore thee!
    As for me and for my children, may we still thy
        realm sustain,
      Roll thine enemies in ruin, bear the shield and
        spear before thee!"

    By this word conciliated, for a space the King
        put by
      All his envious thoughts of David, and relied
        upon his truth;
    So that Michal and her lover dwelt beneath a
        rosy sky,
      In each other's love rejoicing, and their
        golden days of youth.

    And the King made David keeper of the
        borders of the land,
      Where he drubbed the desert raiders, caught
        the robber, killed the beast;
    And the people greatly loved him, for he had
        a generous hand,
      Ready to avenge oppression, or strike harp
        at harvest-feast.

ADULLAM

But young Phaltiel of Gallim went in bitterness
    of mind:
    He had loved the Princess Michal, and had
        wooed her for his wife.
Now he set a watch on David, if some evil he
    might find:
    Some neglect or taint of treason that should
        turn against his life.

Well he knew Saul's native keenness, knew him
    thoughtful and observant,
    And he feared to show his finger in the matter,
        lest he fail:
Saul would reason, "This is Phaltiel—not my
    true and zealous servant
    But the disappointed lover. This is but a
        rival's tale."

So he offered gifts to Doeg—for the man went
    everywhere
    In the business of the cattle, being master
        of the herds—
Saying, "Mark the son of Jesse, and an evil
    rumor bear
    When thou comest to thy master: he will
        hearken to thy words."

And when Doeg came from shearing or from
    numbering the cattle,
    He would speak some word of David, as it
        were a casual thing:
"Thither came the son of Jesse, having triumphed
    in the battle,
    And the people praised him greatly, saying
        he might well be king."

ADULLAM

    Yea, and others brought him whispers—some,
        indeed, in honest zeal,
    But the more in wanton malice or for love of
        Phaltiel's bribes—
    How the son of Jesse plotted, scheming from
        the King to steal
    The allegiance of the people and the scepter
        of the Tribes.

    And these slanders, like a venom, wrought upon
        the mind of Saul
    Till he knew not faith from falsehood, truth
        from treason's blackest dye:
    Had they said his sons and Abner schemed
        with David for his fall,
    Or that Michal brewed him poison, he had
        half believed the lie.

    Therefore Jonathan he summoned: "Seest thou
        not how David keepeth
    Watch against my soul to slay me? 'Tis a
        viper I have fed.
    Therefore arm thine hand against him—stab him
        even while he sleepeth,
    Lest he seize the throne and scepter, take
        the kingdom in my stead."

    But the Prince his friend defended: never yet
        was a commander
    Half so faithful to his sovereign, half so
        valiant, half so wise.
    All that Saul had heard was falsehood, whispered
        rumor, sneaking slander,
    Tittle-tattle of the envious, lies of Phaltiel's
        bribe-bought spies.

ADULLAM

Then the wrath of Saul was kindled, and a
    frenzy more than human
  Shook him as a tree in tempest; like a furnace
    burned his face:
"Know I not how thou dost mock me, son of
    the rebellious woman,
  And hast leagued thyself with David, to thy
    ruin and disgrace?"

So he drave him from his presence, raging
    like a bull of Bashan,
  Shaking roof and walls with curses, till he
    rolled upon the floor—
And his evil spirit found him, weak with wrath
    and spent with passion,
  Entered in and took possession, to depart
    from him no more.

And the nobles of his household looked upon
    the King in sadness,
  Whispering to one another, "Lo, he rages
    uncontrolled.
He will rend us like a lion, tear us piecemeal
    in his madness,
  Save the minstrel, with his harping, charm
    his spirit as of old."

Then did Abner summon David, and the son
    of Jesse hasted,
  And they brought him to the chamber, and
    he stood before the King.
Though his voice was thick with sighing,
    seeing how his lord was wasted,
  Yet the minstrel hid his sorrow, and he
    struck his harp to sing:

ADULLAM

Let quiet have her way: bring not the trumpets
    hither,
  And let the drums depart.
Call not the flutes and viols; only let the
    zither
  Sing to the tired heart.

Let labor be forgot, and tell no tale of
    slaughter
  Nor legend of old wars,
But let the zither sing its song of singing
    water
  And grass and Summer stars.

For there are limpid pools that shine in
    woodland shadows,
  Untroubled, still and deep,
And whispering streams there be that wander
    through the meadows
  Beloved of the sheep.

Their banks are fledged with green of box-tree
    and of myrtle,
  Tall rush and fragrant fern,
And there is heard the song of birds and cooing
    of the turtle
  At April-tide's return.

Bring not the sound of mourning, nor the
    sound of laughter;
  Let pipe and timbrel cease:
But let the zither sing its quiet song, and
    after
  Let there be peace.

For there are hillside pastures, rough with thorn
    and thistle,
  Where roam the flocks at graze,
There flash the swallows' wings, and there the
    cuckoos whistle
  Through Summer's sun-bright days.

And thither come the clouds, like fleets of
    wondrous galleys
  That o'er great ocean pass;
They bring the silvery rain, and clothe the
    thirsting valleys
  With robes of velvet grass.

Yea, all these things our God hath fashioned, and
    He made them
  Most fair for our delight,
That men rejoice in all His works, and hath arrayed
    them
  In robes of day and night.

The Lord that made all these, He slumbereth not
    nor sleepeth.
  The golden spheres that roll
Through heaven, the bird and tree, and all the earth
    He keepeth,
  And He shall keep thy soul.

Then wherefore is thy heart, O King, bowed down
    with anguish?
  Why is thy soul distressed?
Hope thou in God, the Strength and Rock of all
    who languish,
  For He shall give thee rest.

ADULLAM

    Yea, He will keep thee, though they bring no
        vintage hither,
      And drought shall clothe the sod,
    Though herd and harvest fail, and fig and olive
        wither,
      Hope thou in God.

    Whiles he sang, the King sat silent, gnawing at his
        beard and blinking,
      Toying with his ugly javelin, while the music
        filled the hall.
    As a lion eyes his keeper, so he eyed the minstrel,
        thinking,
      "This is he that seeks my kingdom: I will smite
        him to the wall."

    Even as he sat debating, wroth, but half in
        indecision,
      Doubting, while he heard the harping, if his
        rumors were but lies,
    From beneath his couch uncoiling came that viper
        of his vision,
      Never seen before in waking— And its eyes
        were David's eyes.

    As he gazed, the song was ended, and the zither
        ceased its ringing,
      And the minstrel rose from playing—looked on
        Saul and held his breath,
    For the King was dark with anger, with his weapon
        poised for flinging,
      And its stroke was swift as lightning, and its
        point was keen as death.

"Traitor of the House of Jesse! Shameless even in
    thy shame!
    Angel-eyed and serpent-hearted! Take the final
        gift of Saul!"
But a harp-string turned the weapon, or his fury
    marred his aim,
    For the dart grazed David's shoulder, and struck
        quivering in the wall.

All amazed to see him scatheless, and in doubt if
    he were mortal,
    Saul cried out, "An hundred shekels to the man
        that strikes him dead!
Will ye let him go, ye traitors?"— David leaped and
    reached the portal,
    Flung aside the guards that seized him, vanished
        through the gate, and fled.

—Fled among the whispering olives, with the
    runners hot behind him,
    Sped across the field and vineyard, and flew
        panting up the height;
Plunged into a thorny thicket where the hunters
    could not find him
    Though they beat the woods around him:
        there he lay till fall of night.

II

So David fled from Saul, and went his way
To Samuel at Rama. Sere and gray
The Prophet was, for age had wasted him,
And sorrowing for Saul. His eye was dim,
His body nibbled by the teeth of care
Until he might have vanished into air
Or floated on the wind, so like a wraith
He seemed. Yet still he held the torch of Faith

ADULLAM

For them that followed, so the living Light
Should not be quenched again in heathen night;
And while he tarried, waiting for his end,
He gathered younger prophets to attend
Upon his words, that they might learn the ways
Of God, and show His will to coming days.

Here David told his tale. The ancient saint
Heard even to the end his sore complaint
With patience, as a kindly man will hark
To sobbings of a child that dreads the dark,
Who knows no harm is near, and yet can feel
The aching of the hurt he may not heal.
He said, "Abide, until the Lord hath shown
What He will have thee do." He too had known
The King's malignity: had he not lost
The holy things he loved, because he crossed
The will of Saul? And yet his gentle eyes
Held no resentment, but a radiance wise
And sweet with peace. A lion for the Lord,
He knew not fear of men, and would have warred
With giants in His service; in his own
He would not strive. The Ark and altar-stone
He yielded to the Priest, at Saul's command,
Gave up the hallowed vessels to his hand,
And waited for his end in peace. The Lord
Was yet his shield, his hope and his reward.

He called his servant now to wash the feet
Of David, set before him bread and meat,
And said again, "Till God make known His will
Abide thou here, for He will keep thee still."
So David tarried, till the hue and cry
That shook the land with tumult had gone by;
Then Samuel bade him, "Go, return, and seek
Prince Jonathan thy friend, and he shall speak

Of thee unto the King; and if he will
Entreat thee kindly, thou shalt serve him still
And seek his peace. If not, the land is wide,
With holds and fastnesses where thou mayest hide;
And thou shalt trust the Lord, nor be afraid
What man can do to thee." Thereon he laid
His shrunken hand on David's head, like one
Who gives his blessing to an only son,
And wept and kissed him, saying, "I shall see
Thy face no more. But God hath chosen thee
For mighty things— In city and in den
To be a captain over dauntless men,
And they shall serve thee. Yet, when thou art strong,
Take heed thou use thy greatness not in wrong,
Remembering that the stranger and the poor
Are sent of God, and all who must endure
Oppression: these are His. And in the days
When thou art mighty, neither shalt thou raise
Thine hand against the King, nor draw a sword
To spill his blood—not even though the Lord
Shall set him in thine hand. God made him King,
And thou shalt do him honor, lest thou bring
God's wrath upon thee. Cleave not to his foes
Nor vex his friends; but be a help to those
Who have no help—the wronged and dispossessed.
The Lord hath blessed thee; and thou shalt be blessed."

Then David went again, and found his friend
The son of Saul, where he had gone to bend
His bow and strike the target, being a strong
And cunning archer. And he asked, "What wrong
Hath David done? What evil hath been found
In him, that Saul's swift hunters scour the ground
To take his soul? Wherein do I offend?
If there be wickedness in David, end
My life thyself. If I be innocent,

ADULLAM

Then tell me why thy father is intent
To shed my blood?"

The Prince made hot reply:
"My father hath not willed that thou shouldst die.
Thou knowest his curse: it was the nameless thing
That kennels in his brain, and not the King
That cast the dart. All this my father told
To me that day, while down his cheeks there rolled
Hot tears of anguish—how his madness came
Like midnight on him, and he did thee shame,
Unwitting what he did. He rues the deed
With boundless grief. His runners went at speed
To bring thee back again, that he might show
To thee his loving favor. Lo, I know
My father's counsels: be they great or small
He hides them not from me. And why should Saul
Desire thy death? Be sure that if he did
His son should know it. Why should this be hid
From Jonathan? And let the powers on high
Bear witness of my falsehood if I lie."

And David said, "I know thee true, my Prince,
As God Himself; and well thou mightest convince
A man who never heard that javelin sing:
I heard its message, and I know the King
Hath sworn my doom. He knoweth well the love
And favor thou hast shown thy friend—whereof
I am unworthy—therefore doth he leave
His counsels secret, lest his son should grieve.
But, as God liveth, and as thou hast breath,
I swear I never stood so nigh to death
As in this hour. If thou dost love me, seek
The presence of the King, and thou shalt speak
To him of David, saying, 'Yester-eve
The man besought me, and I gave him leave

To go from Gibeah, that he might return
To Bethlehem his city, where they burn
The yearly sacrifice'—and if it be
That he shall seem unmoved, and answer thee
' 'Tis well,' thy servant shall have peace. But mark
If he shall redden, if his brow grow dark,
His hand steal toward his dagger, or he grind
His teeth together—evil is designed
Against my life. As shepherds scan the sky
At morn and eve, to know if storms be nigh,
So watch thy father's face and learn his will,
And bring me tidings, be they good or ill."

And Jonathan replied, "Doth not the moon
Come new to-morrow night? And thou shalt soon
Be missed, thy place being empty. Then will I,
If Saul shall ask of thee, make such reply
As thou hast bidden. I will mark the King,
And if he pass it as a little thing,
It shall be well with thee; but if he burn
In anger, I shall know it. So we learn
His will to thee. Meantime, do thou remain
Beside this rock, until I come again.
And come I will, as oft I do, to bend
My bow at random marks. And when I send
The lad to fetch the arrows, I will cry
Behind, as if to tell him where they lie.
And if I say, 'Behold, the arrows fell
Behind thee,' thou shall know that all is well
And there is peace to thee. But if I say,
'The arrows lie beyond thee'—Go thy way,
For God hath sent thee hence. And may the Lord
Blot out my name if I shall break my word.
And as for me, behold, the Lord hath seen
Mine innocence. Jehovah be between
Thy house and mine henceforth; and when I sleep
Among my fathers, thou shalt surely keep

ADULLAM

This peace of God to those I leave behind
Forever; neither let it cross thy mind
To cut them off, not even when the hand
Of God cuts off forever from the land
Thine enemies."

                    He went, and David hid
That day and all the following day amid
The boulders of the field, and vexed his brain
With thoughts of Michal. Was it all in vain
His days were spent in labor, and his nights
In watching for the foe from lonely heights,
This many a year, that he might have for prize
The King's fair daughter with her starry eyes?
And must he lose her now? And why had Saul
Grown strange to him? He watched the slow sun crawl
Across the sky: with slender silver bow
The moon stole down the quiet afterglow
To hide behind the hills, and then the skies
Grew thick with stars, that shone like Michal's eyes,
And from her window in the wall there shone
The light that said, "My heart is David's own."—
The lamp that Michal never failed to light
When he was absent. In the vast of night
That cloaked the world, how clear and bright its burning,
Like faith through doubt. And many a time, returning
Belated, he had caught its gleam afar
Against the dark, a splendid, new-made star,
To guide his footsteps home. He felt the air
Grow sweet as with her breath, and breathed a prayer
That God might keep her safe and keep her true
Through all adversity. Thereon he drew
His mantle close, and, crouched beneath a thorn,
He watched the candle fade into the morn.

At last came Jonathan, with bow in hand
And quiver at his back, and took his stand
Not far from David's hiding-place, among

ADULLAM

The clumps of stunted thorn. He bent and strung
The stubborn weapon, drew, and loosed the string,
And David heard the feathered arrow sing
High overhead. Then twice again he drew,
And twice the hissing shafts took wing, and flew
Birdlike in air. Then to his lad he said,
"Go, now, and fetch the arrows I have sped."
And while he ran, the Prince sent forth a cry
Behind him: "Lo, do not the arrows lie
Beyond thee? Speed, make haste and tarry not!
They fell beyond!" And when the stripling got
The shafts and brought them, Jonathan unstrung
His bow, and to the lad his weapons flung,
And bade him take them home. So, unaware
Of what had passed, he left his master there,
And hastened blithely home.

                        And as he ran
He met the fox-faced Shimei, a man
That served the King; one readier to hear
Than speak his thoughts, and skilled to lay his ear
To chamber doors. If any plucked the sleeve
Of one that passed, the fellow would perceive
And follow them apart; so men had learned
To shun his narrow eyes, and he had earned
The name of Weasel. Seeing the boy, he slipped
Behind a thorn, and waited there, tight-lipped,
Till he had passed him by. The lad, intent
On supper, marked him not, and onward went,
Rattling the quiver, wondering why the son
Of Saul left off his practice, scarce begun,
And why he lingered in the field alone.

Then David came from hiding by the stone
And flung himself upon his face, and bowed
Before the Prince, and both lamented loud;
And neither one (for both with tears were blind)
Saw Shimei the spy steal close behind

ADULLAM

To hearken to their speech. Enwrapped in woe
They heard him not. And David said, "I know
All pleasant things are past; all peace is done.
I am become an outlaw, and as one
From men cut off, and none for me shall mourn."
His friend made answer, "Lo, we both have sworn
That God shall be between us, and our seed
Forever. Go: Jehovah be thy speed,
Thy safety and thy peace." And David said,
"What peace is left to me? Henceforth I tread
The ways of bitterness, afar from thee
And all I love. Behold, my wife shall be
A stranger to my heart. Yet once, before
I go my way, though giants keep her door,
I swear to see her face. The soul of man
Is but a vapor, and his life a span.
Yea, man is like a flower that blooms at dawn:
The hot winds pass, he withereth, and is gone.
Then wherefore hoard my life, or shun the spears
That seek my soul? Before me lie the years
As bleak as Winter and as dry as dust,
And all mine honor is a beggar's crust.
Were this a thing to treasure?—but to feel
Her breath upon my cheek, her white arms steal
Around my shoulders—though the swords of Saul
That instant slew me, this I should recall
To time's last hour, and it should make the tomb
Smell sweet as wind-swept leagues of Summer bloom."

Then said the friends farewell, embraced and kissed;
And Jonathan, like one that gropes through mist
Nor sees the path before him, slowly paced
Through those dun fields, by Winter's hands laid waste,
And came to Gibeah. And the lurking spy
Followed afar, with crafty step and eye,
And sought for Phaltiel and told his tale.
And Phaltiel armed his guard with spears and mail.

III

Though Happiness forget, yet still Despair remembers.
    With trembling hand she tends her slowly fading fire:
The ash of olden hopes, where chilled and blackening embers
    No more can warm desire.

The yellowing woods are hers, where leaf and blossom wither;
    The lichen-fretted tomb; the wreck upon the shore;
Gray deserts of the soul, with paths that run nowhither,
    Where hope returns no more.

Strange treasures these to keep; and Happiness is wiser
    Who spends with lavish hand her splendors ere they wane.
But gray Despair is mad, who hoardeth like a miser
    The things that hold but pain.

So David nursed his grief, in dark Adullam's kennel,
    And kept that evening hour upon the wintry wold:
The salty taste of tears, the smell of trampled fennel,
    The sunset's tarnished gold;

Familiar sounds grown strange—the lowing of the cattle,
    The shout of boys at play, the single trumpet-blare;
Far off, like Titan laughter, the guard-drum's sullen rattle
    That mocked at his despair;

And then the deepening dusk, when stars began to glitter
    And happier men turned home to wife and roof and fire,
And sheep were safely folded. His heart grew black and bitter
    With anguish and desire.

The frost was in his marrow: an icy wind came creeping
    Across the withered grass, and he was fain to die.
And with her silver sickle the slender moon came reaping
    The harvest of the sky.

ADULLAM

And then, to prick his heart with wild and restless yearning,
    A new-created star upon the breast of night,
Against the dark he saw the lamp of Michal burning,
    A golden rose of light.

So still her love shone forth: let life roll on, full cycle,
    And still let faith be bright, though other lights were few!
Not even the power of Saul should rob him of his Michal:
    That death alone could do!

What matter though the swords of Phaltiel's hirelings found him?
    What though the King himself kept ward before her door?
Far better that he die, with Michal's arms around him,
    Than see her face no more.

Yea, men, for women's love, had matched their might with giants,
    Had entered hostile holds, disdaining tower and wall.
Then should not he, for Michal, bid Phaltiel defiance
    And dare the wrath of Saul?

He set his face toward home, as turns the eagle nestward,
    And darker, as he went, around him closed the night
With shuddering terrors thronged; but the pale moon to westward
    Shed faint, illusive light.

He passed the leafless vines, and then the olives darkened
    His path with deepening shade. He all but held his breath,
For fears beset him hard; but when he paused and harkened
    The world was still as death.

No sound but murmurous leaves, and whispering of the water
    That seethed beneath its banks, the squeak of bat or mole.
But in those shades might lurk bright daggers, bare for slaughter,
    And keen to spill his soul.

ADULLAM

He crossed the olive grove; the wall rose blank before him.
    An hundred wars of old had seamed its face with scars;
Yet still it mocked his hope. And the wide heaven rolled o'er him,
    Gleaming with frosty stars.

Let gates be barred with brass: they may be wrenched asunder.
    Let walls reach high as heaven: the high heart climbs the stone.
Hedge loveliness with spears and circle her with thunder:
    Desire will find his own.

The gate was shut and barred; but under Michal's casement
    A vine had scaled the wall, with roots that sucked the stones:
A perilous place to climb, amid that wild enlacement:
    A slip would break his bones.

As one that dreams he clomb, with sinewy fingers twining.
    The rough vines tore his hands: he did not know nor care.
Before him swam her eyes, like stars at even shining,
    Through clouds of dusky hair.

Her hair was thick with dusk, and her look held no denial;
    Her hands were clasped in his; her eyes were soft with tears.
Her voice, like the sigh of winds or the low, deep tones of a viol,
    Was calling in his ears.

Then came the wintry wind, with a roar like the roar of a lion,
    And shook him there as he clung, as a hound the hare in his teet
The sky was a whirl of stars—Wild Taurus and great Orion,
    And the earth spun round beneath.

Sick and dizzy he clung, with the wind around him streaming.
    The window seemed but a star, a thousand leagues in the sky.
If death were an end of pain, a slumber that knew no dreaming,
    Then why should he dread to die?

ADULLAM

But oh, his dearly beloved! Only again to behold her,
   To feel her hands on his head, and her heart against his side,
To say, "I love thee," again, and pillow his head on her shoulder
   But once, before he died!

And then... did she lean above him, sweet and lovely and tender,
   So near he could feel her breath and hear the beat of her blood?
His fears were scattered abroad like bats by the sunrise splendor:
   Life surged in his heart like a flood.

White arms reached down to embrace him. Her voice was the
     voice of a lyre:
   "Beloved!" she cried, "Beloved!" And easy it was to win
A hold on the ledge of the window, borne up on the wings of
     desire.
   And Michal drew him within.

She clasped and clung to him close, her dark hair rippling around
     him.
   She loosed his girdle and sword, and his mantle, drenched with
     the dew.
"Lo, it is David, my lover! Honor and glory have crowned him!
   I knew he would come: I knew."

Then she had flown like a bird, and left him perplexed and
     forsaken,
   But soon she returned with a pitcher and clusters of raisins
     fine,
A bellows to blow the brazier, and wafers with honey baken,
   And warmed him a cup of wine.

"Rest, my beloved," she prayed, "with my arm for a pillow
     under
   The dewy locks of thy hair, and look on me with cheer."
And David ate and drank, and his heart grew warm with wonder
   To feel his love so near.

"Oh would to God," she said, "I were some poor man's daughter!
   So might my lord be safe from danger and from dole!
The King, with lifted hand, hath doomed thee to the slaughter:
   His warriors hunt thy soul.

"Go, hide thee in some den, and let my soul bewail thee,
   Until his heart shall change, his wrath be overpast.
Jehovah keep thee safe, His mercy never fail thee,
   And bring thee back at last."

But whiles she spake, there came a crash of spear-butts grounded,
   A tramp of sandaled feet, the beat of mail-clad hands
Upon the door below; and Phaltiel's shout resounded:
   "Unbar! The King commands!"

And David said, "My sword; and let me front the traitor.
   As he hath been my curse, so I will be his doom.
Though girt with mail he come, yet by the Great Creator,
   This place shall be his tomb!"

"Nay, nay, but fly!" she cried, "for even though thou slay him
   His guards will cut thee down, and leave me but despair.
Ah God! The porter opens: no mortal power can stay him!
   Their tread is on the stair!"

She dragged him to the window. One thought she had—one only:
   The swords were at the door, the swords of Phaltiel's men!
His lips burned hot on hers: how oft, in midnights lonely,
   She dreamed that kiss again!

She gave him to the dark, the thrashing vines, the glitter
   Of stars; then turned again to view the vacant room:
A place of memories, now, and yearning bleak and bitter—
   The shadow of a tomb.

And when before their thrust the door burst from its hinges,
   And Phaltiel and his guards into her chamber poured,
She lay on David's cloak, and kissed its purple fringes
   And his forgotten sword.

ADULLAM

IV

Now, in those days, Ahimelech the Priest
  Had brought the Tabernacle and the Ark
To Nob. For Samuel's years were far increased:
  His stumbling feet went slipping down the dark
Lone way to death; and Saul had found excuse
  In this to set another in his stead,
To sacrifice according to the use,
  And dress the table with its hallowed bread.

A worthy man, both loyal to the Lord
  And Saul the King; as open as a door,
As honest as a dog, he duly poured
  The offerings of wine, and took no more
Of hallowed things than Moses' Law declared
  His meed: the thigh, the shoulder and the breast;
And these with all who served he duly shared,
  To each his part. The fire consumed the rest.

He saw no deeper than the crust of things.
  No high, prophetic visions came to him:
He never caught the flash of seraph-wings
  Nor heard the shouting of the cherubim.
In all things faithful, but intense in none,
  He fed the fire and slew the sacrifice,
And touched the hallowed vessels, one by one,
  As merchants move amid their merchandise.

To him came David, on a wintry morn
  When frost lay thick as ashes on the mould
And birds sat pinched and shivering in the thorn.
  His panting breath smoked white against the cold,
For hot with haste he came, and weaponless,
  Bleak-faced and haggard, stealing backward looks
As fearing what might follow; and his dress
  Was marred with dirt and torn with bramble-hooks.

ADULLAM

Then went the Priest to meet him, and his face
   Was pale (for saving Saul and Jonathan
No man in Israel held higher place
   Or wielded greater power than Jesse's son),
And asked, "Why comest thou alone, my Lord,
   And no man with thee? Hath there been a fight
And Israel smitten? Is thy bodyguard
   Cut off or slain? Hath Saul been put to flight?"

Two years had David moved among the lies
   And tricks and treacheries that thrive at court,
Where being smooth meant more than being wise,
   And speaking truth was deemed a fool's resort.
But something lingered yet of that uncouth
   And rugged honesty that men instill
Who guard their sheep from wolves, and speak the truth,
   And keep the plighted word, befall what will.

And now he all but blurted out the fact
   That he was outlawed and a fugitive
From Saul's vindictive malice; that he lacked
   Both food and arms, and prayed the Priest to give
His aid and counsel. But the ready lie
   Lay nigh at hand—and yonder, like a toad,
Old Doeg sat, Saul's slaughterman and spy.
   What fiend had set this viper in his road?

He knew the man: a captive out of Edom,
   A brand the King had plucked from out the fire
Of war, and afterward had given him freedom;
   Yet still he served, because he loved his hire.
And at his master's bidding, he would do
   Such infamies as even soldiers tell
With pallid lips; a villain through and through,
   A devil, gendered at the stud of Hell.

ADULLAM

And David felt that pricking of the hair
  Of one who flees along a precipice
In dreams when lo, the crag is turned to air,
  And sends him hurtling down some vast abyss.
For so an empty belly oft will make
  The high heart faint, and foul the spirit bold
With sickening terrors, even as a snake
  Beslimes the bird that soared through heaven of old.

He swallowed back the truth, and spake the lie
  That doomed the Priest to death, though wavering
Before the herdman's cold and sullen eye:
  "I have a secret errand for the King.
My men await me in the torrent-bed
  Beyond the town—a small and chosen band—
And faint we are. I pray thee give us bread,
  Or whatsoever food thou hast at hand."

The whiles he spake, the Priest stood blinking fast
  With puffed and watery eyes, his fingers twined
In grizzled beard; for though no shadow passed
  Of doubt of David's words across his mind,
He found himself as one who hath two friends,
  Both high in place, whose interests oppose;
And whatsoe'er he doeth, he offends
  At least the one, or makes them both his foes.

"My Lord, no common bread is here," he said,
  "Naught save the loaves that God hath set aside
For His own house, the Consecrated Bread.
  Yet if thy men be clean and purified..."
He paused, and blinked again in hesitation:
  "Thou knowest the Lord is jealous of His own.
Thou knowest well the Bread of Presentation
  Is lawful for the priests to eat alone."

ADULLAM

But David asked, "Was not the manna holy
   God sent our fathers from His place on high?
Yet all partook, the mighty with the lowly,
   Both priests and people, and they did not die.
My men are clean: they have been kept from women
   These past three days; their bags are holy now.
The need is sore. May not thy bread be common
   To us, who serve the Lord no less than thou?"

Ahimelech reasoned that the Lord was far,
   And might not mark him; but the King was nigh,
Implacable and fierce, with men of war,
   Unlikely to forgive should he deny
His own ambassador and son-in-law,
   Who wore the royal turban on his head.
So, half in charity and half in awe,
   He yielded, and brought forth the hallowed bread;

And said, "Lo, Doeg, who hath come to bring
   The bullocks for the altar, he is nigh
To see how I have rendered to the King
   The hallowed things that gold could never buy.
And he is witness how I bow beneath
   My Lord the King's command, nor contravene
His will." And Doeg, through his crooked teeth,
   Made answer, "I am witness: I have seen."

Then David questioned, "Hast thou weapons here?
   The King's commandment brooked of no delay,
And all in haste I came, without my spear
   Nor even a sword." Ahimelech answered, "Yea,
Goliath's sword is here, that mighty blade
   Thou slewest him with, laid up before the Lord."
And David answered, "Let me be arrayed
   With that. I know not of a better sword."

ADULLAM

    Ahimelech girt him with it, as he asked,
        And blessed his errand, wishing him success
    And safe and swift return; and Doeg masked
        His malice under seeming friendliness,
    The whiles his slow, reptilian mind took note
        Of every word and action, conning all,
    As simple men commit a tale by rote,
        That he might tell it in the ears of Saul.

    And all that day did David flee, and through
        The coming night, and half another day,
    While ever as he fled his terrors grew,
        Till every field and thicket by the way
    Seemed thronged with spears. Like Ishmael he stood
        Against the world: all weapons were unsheathed
    To drink his life; all Israel sought his blood,
        And nothing was his friend that moved or breathed.

    But what was his offence? He did not know:
        The King's delight had been to honor him
    And give him gifts; what made him now his foe?
        His ears yet tingled at the memory grim
    Of that last time he sang before the King,
        The sudden fury in the eyes of Saul,
    And even yet he heard the javelin sing
        That pinned his broidered mantle to the wall.

    Then came his hasty flight, and his return
        To Jonathan, that ever was his friend:
    The Prince had taken life in hand to learn
        What sin was his, and how he might amend
    His case with Saul; and he had lain concealed
        Till Jonathan brought word the King had vowed
    His death; and they had parted in the field
        With pledge of faith, and both had wept aloud.

ADULLAM

And he had gone in jeopardy of life
   To his own house, to keep a final tryst
And bid farewell unto his gentle wife,
   The star-eyed Michal. Even while they kissed
And clung had come a thunder at the gate
   Of grounded spears; then Michal weeping sore
With fear; and then his flight—almost too late—
   With Phaltiel's soldiers hammering at the door.

So David mourned, believing he had lost
   His wife forever, and his faithful friend.
What profited his life at such a cost?
   Though he should live till doomsday, he would spend
His days in grief until the world should wither.
   And Saul— He loved him still, in spite of all
Injustice. Never more should he strike zither
   To charm the King, nor draw his sword for Saul.

And, sorrowing so, at last he found a den
   In wild Adullam, where a slender brook,
Slow-trickling from the cavern, clothed a glen
   With willow trees and rushes. Here he took
His lodging, like a wild and hunted thing,
   And roamed abroad by night, but hid his face
From daylight, while the runners of the King
   Combed all the land to find his hiding-place.

Abigail

I

Abigail the fair was the wife of Nabal.
He was old and ugly; she was young and kind.
He loved roasted mutton smoking on the table,
    She the ewes in April grass, with their lambs behind.

Shunned of men was he, by his thralls detested;
    Having great possessions, he held them like a churl.
Soft of word was she, ripe and ample-breasted,
    Matronly in face and form; in her heart a girl.

Wrinkled though he was, past the warmth of passion,
    Still his temper burnt like a smouldering coal.
Cheerfully she served him, and in wifely fashion,
    Yet her soul recoiled from his ugly soul.

Grassy meads were his, fertile fields for reaping,
    Sheep and kine and asses, barn and byre and fold.
Hard was he in getting, harder still in keeping,
    Hoarding wool and barley as miser does his gold.

Nabal was a knave, Nabal was a glutton,
    Nabal was a niggard, loving wealth and ease;
Rich in vine and olive, corn and beef and mutton,
    Gave he not in charity the paring of a cheese.

They that sought his aid found him hard and sordid:
    "Many servants break from their masters now-a-days.
Shall I take of that which my care hath hoarded
    To bestow on worthless knaves begging by the ways?

"Ye—to eat my bread, feast upon my marrow!
  Hence, before your hides pay your folly's tax!
Get you back to bondage, to the plough and harrow,
  Ere ye feel the cudgels of my shepherds on your backs!

"Ye shall have of mine neither sup nor swallow.
  Get you from my doors, and get you from my lands."—
If occasion offered, Abigail would follow,
  Saying, "Take, I pray you now, a blessing at my hands."

So men spake of Nabal with hissing and with curses;
  So the name of Nabal a household oath became:
But the gentle Abigail ever dealt in mercies:
  All the homeless loved her, and the hungry blessed her
    name.

II

Now David dwelt in exile, and there drew
Around him all the outlawed and oppressed,
The debtor and the poor, and such as knew
Injustice, and the wronged and dispossessed;
For those were days when many were distressed,
And virtue languished, and oppression grew.

So day by day there gathered to his side
To be his liegemen those of might and worth,
Too proud to brook Saul's overweening pride,
Too just to watch while honesty and mirth
Were trod in dust, and outrage walked the earth—
Such men as dared not live where honor died.

And some were such as might have rocked the throne
Of Saul himself, had David given consent,
Renowned in battle. Had the trumpet blown
For war with Saul, doubt not that they had rent
His regal ensign from the battlement
And leveled Gibeah to its corner-stone.

ABIGAIL

    But David was their leader and their law,
    Whom all obeyed; and though his soul abhorred
    The deeds of Saul, no weapon would he draw
    Against the man anointed of the Lord,
    But kept the borders safe, and only warred
    With desert thieves, and held the King in awe.

    Now Saul had learnt from Doeg of the aid
    To David given by the Priest at Nob;
    The gift of hallowed bread, the giant's blade—
    And cried, with all his seething blood athrob,
    "Though these be priests of God who dare to rob
    The house of Saul, they yet shall be repaid!

    "Arise, ye servants of the King, and smite
    Ahimelech's house with fury. Blot his name
    From under heaven, for his hand has plight
    With Jesse's son. Let infamy and shame
    His portion be: let steel and burning flame
    Root out this den of vipers from my sight!"

    And when his vassals feared to lift their hand
    Against the priests, and smite the holy place,
    He said to Doeg, "Go, array thy band
    And do my will. Thou fearest not the face
    Of God Himself; for thou art of the race
    Of Edom: therefore do as I command."

    Then Doeg fell on Nob with sword and fire,
    And butchered the inhabitants like sheep,
    Trampling its thoroughfares to bloody mire,
    And left the city but a ruinous heap
    Of desolations: none was left to weep
    Within the walls, and none to feel desire;

ABIGAIL

But only fire-gnawed timbers, crumbling stones,
And sword-gashed bodies in disorder piled—
Abominations that the day disowns
And night abhors—all bloody and defiled,
Where ravens flapped, and jackals from the wild
Stole forth to rend the flesh and crunch the bones.

Yet one escaped: Abiathar, the son
Of the High Priest Ahimelech. He fled
And came to David's hold at set of sun;
And men beheld his garments stained with red
As from the wine-press; and he bowed his head
In bitterness, and told what Saul had done:

"They clave my father's hoary head before
The hallowed altar. On the threshold stone
They spilt my mother's life, and shed the gore
Of wife and children. I am left alone
To walk the world in sorrow for mine own,
And beg for strangers' bread from door to door."

And David, looking through his tortured eyes,
Beheld his soul a desert where no rain
Shall fall henceforth, nor any flower arise
To cheer the heart; but there is endless pain,
And naught but anguish and despair remain,
Like ruined towers, black against the skies.

He bowed his face: "I saw it in the day
That Doeg met me at the temple gate.
Yea, even then, I knew he would betray
Thy father's blood to Saul's unpitying hate.
Lo, I have brought upon thee such a weight
Of grief as tears can never wash away.

ABIGAIL

"Abide thou here, if yet thou canst forgive
The evil I have done thee. They that seek
Thy life seek mine as well: but thou mayest live
In safeguard here, for David is not weak,
But mighty men obey me when I speak,
Though I be outlawed and a fugitive."

The other answered, "Yea, since thou art kind,
And pitiest the poor and the distressed;
Though all that I have loved is left behind
In blood and ashes, let me here find rest,
And I will be thy Priest. God manifest
His grace to thee, and show thee all His mind."

And so the Priest abode, and builded there
An altar from the boulders of the field,
And ministered with incense and with prayer
And daily sacrifice. But Saul appealed
To Heaven in vain, for there was none that healed
Or heard, or that regarded his despair.

So long, indeed, the King had trod the track
Which he had chosen in his pride of mind,
That though destruction gathered fierce and black
Before his face, and ruin stretched behind
Like ash of smitten cities, he could find
No penitence nor place of turning back.

On then, in darkness! Even though he hears
Abaddon rising like a sullen sea
Until her billows thunder in his ears,
He turns not from his purpose. The decree
Full well he knows, yet will not bow the knee,
Though heaven itself should fill with clanging spears.

ABIGAIL

He hears the peoples all around him seethe
With wrath and tumult: Edom hath rebelled,
While Moab arms, and Zobah's trumpets breathe
Their bronze defiance. But the sword that held
The tribes in terror and their turmoils quelled
Shall David for the King no more unsheathe?

Yea, where is David? For thy people's sake,
O Saul, speak yet the word that shall regain
The help of him whose shout was wont to shake
The field of war! Alas, the hope is vain—
Let anger work his will and pride remain,
Though honor perish and the kingdom break!

He summons him he deems his staunchest friend,
The faithless Phaltiel: "Shall my daughter still
Be joined to him I hate, who will not bend
To my commands, and ever plots my ill?
This day shall Michal wed thee, ere I fill
Mine eyes with sleep, although the world should end!"

The shameful preparations move apace:
The minstrels touch their harps; the wine is poured.
A stunned amazement looks from every face,
But Saul is King, and will not be implored;
And David's wife must wed another lord,
In hated bonds, adulterous and base.

They fetch the bride, and tearlessly she comes,
Though white as ashes. Merab's eyes are red
With grief, and Jonathan in anger thumbs
His dagger-hilt; but none hath hardihead
To cry, "For shame!" The festal board is spread,
The trumpets peal, and there is roll of drums.

ABIGAIL

The smoking torches flicker in the gust
Of darkening streets; the flowery garlands swing
In odorous airs. Lay joy and peace in dust,
O daughter of the King! The minstrels sing
But dirges, and the bride's attendants wring
Their hands, beholding beauty wed to lust.

They reach the bridegroom's house: the horrid door
Swings wide in welcome. Whither shall she turn,
What set her hope upon, or whom implore?
Ah God, must she, the wife of David, learn
To bear the shames and infamies that earn
The wretched, bitter wages of the whore?

The pitiless doors have closed upon the place,
And Michal is imprisoned with despair
And her new lord. The beauty and the grace
That once were David's—hands and lips and hair—
All these doth Phaltiel claim; and she must bare
Her milk-white loveliness to his embrace.

Yea, she is wed to him—if one be wed
Who yields to alien arms a bitter breast
That once was pillow for a dearer head,
Who hungers still for fingers that caressed
Her hair in happier days, the heart that pressed
Against her own, and there was comforted.

Yet memory keeps a refuge from despair;
A watered garden, where her soul may meet
With David, and they walk together there
Through deeps of shadowy olive wood, made sweet
With song of nightingales, while hearts and feet
Move side by side, and love is ever fair.

ABIGAIL

So Michal dreams, and half forgets the smart
Of Phaltiel's loathed caresses, and the wrong
Of lawless wedlock, while she dwells apart
With him she loves. His arms are sweet and strong
Around her there; his voice is like a song;
His head lies warm and heavy on her heart.

III

Saul the King is hunting: there are trumpets in the
  North;
 Let the lion seek the covert, let the leopard keep
  his den!
He hath girt the sword upon him and the cry is
  streaming forth—
 Saul the King is gone a-hunting with three
  thousand chosen men.

Saul the King is hunting: through the hills of
  Benjamin
 There is gleam of helm and harness and a shaking
  forth of flags;
Past the ancient fort of Jebus rolls the rumor and the
  din,
 There are curses in the thickets, there are shouts
  among the crags.

Saul the King is hunting, and his dogs are on the
  trail;
 Bethlehem beholds the morning fill with flash of
  sword and spear;
Gallim hears the creak of wagons and the tread of
  men in mail—
 Saul the King is gone a-hunting, but he doth not
  hunt the deer.

ABIGAIL

Saul the King is hunting after David and his men!
  All the mountains shake with shouting and the
      highway smokes beneath,
  For his heart is hot with fury, and he will not turn
      again:
  Saul hath drawn the sword of vengeance, and
      hath cast away the sheath.

Saul the King is hunting: he will trample and
    consume.
  Meronoth hath seen the lances like the dawn
      against the sky.
  Tarry not, O Son of Jesse, lest Adullam be thy
      tomb!
  Gedor hears the tramp of footmen as the hunt
      goes sweeping by.

Linger not among the shepherds, nor beside the
    threshing-floors:
  Get thee to the barren uplands where the goat
      and leopard roam.
  Fly the King, as flees the roebuck when the hungry
      lion roars:
  Let the desert be thy safety, and the wilderness
      thy home.

Saul the King is hunting: on through Mamre
    sweeps the chase,
  Where the Lord held talk with Abram, face to
      face and eye to eye;
  Past the hoary walls of Debir, where, to win a
      woman's grace,
  Othniel smote the sons of Anak in their holds
      against the sky.

Tarry not, O Son of Jesse, for the sword of wrath
     is bare!
  Onward through the hills of Judah move the
     huntsmen like a flood;
And the King will have no mercy, neither will his
     sworders spare,
  For their trampling shakes the valleys and their
     lances thirst for blood.

Enter not the gates of Hebron; though the felon
     there may find
  Refuge, when the blood-avenger follows him
     with fury shod:
There for thee is none asylum; for the King is hot
     behind,
  And hath bade his warriors slay thee at the
     altar-stone of God.

Saul the King is hunting through the Wilderness
     of Ziph:
  Jesse's son hath fled before him, and he can no
     farther flee;
For behind him close the hunters, and before him
     drops the cliff:
  He is trapped among the headlands, by the bitter,
     tideless sea.

Saul the King is hunting; and his trumpets' brazen
     throats
  Soon shall sing aloud of triumph, for the hunt is
     nigh its end.
David's men are in a cavern near the Fountain of
     the Goats,
  And their doom is hard upon them, save the Lord
     Himself defend.

ABIGAIL

    Down the stony way from Maon comes the trample
        and the shout:
      So the blood-devouring weasel tracks the coney
        to his nest.
    David's men lie spent and breathless while the
        huntsmen pass without,
      But the King discerns the cavern, and he enters
        in to rest.

    And around his fret and fever fall the shadows,
        cool and deep,
      While the outlaws fiercely whisper, "Now
        behold the reckoning hour!
    Doubting not of danger near him, see him stretch
        himself to sleep.
      Lo, Jehovah hath delivered him that hates thee to
        thy power!"

    Groaning, David steals upon him, draws the dagger
        from his sheath,
      Pauses, blade uplifted, peering at that visage of
        despair,
    With its brows like shaggy thickets shadowing the
        eyes beneath,
      Sunken cheek and wrinkled forehead, wreathed
        with slowly graying hair.

    For the fragrant wind of memory brings a breath of
        olden years
      When the King had showed him kindness, and
        he stands with trembling hand:
    "Who art thou, O Son of Jesse, outlawed chief of
        robber spears?
      Wilt thou slay the Lord's anointed—smite the
        ruler of the land?"

ABIGAIL

Then come thoughts of star-eyed Michal: groaning
    in his heart anew,
  Shrinking from the impious action, David by his
    master kneels,
Gently from the sleeper's mantle rips the broidered
    fringe of blue,
  Sheathes again the bloodless dagger; back to his
    companions steals.

Then a murmur swells among them: "God hath
    brought to thee thy foe:
  And thy hand hath spared the tyrant, still to slay,
    oppress and rob!
Thou hast looked on him with mercy—him that
    worketh Israel woe!
  Think of all the wrongs we suffer, and the
    guiltless blood of Nob."

David answers, "God forbid it, that my hand
    should do this thing!
  God forgive me that I touched him, that I
    marred his garment's hem.
Smite the chosen of Jehovah? Lift mine hand
    against the King?
  This is he that bears the scepter, he that wears the
    diadem!"

In the quiet of the even, when the dusk is gathering
    gray,
  Folding all the earth in shadows softer than the
    night-moth's wing,
Saul has wakened from his slumber, and departs
    upon his way.
  David follows close behind him, crying out, "My
    Lord the King!"

ABIGAIL

>   Then the King turns back in wonder, asking, "Who
>   is this that cries?
>   Turn and look upon him, Abner, for I think our
>   search is done.
>   Is it not my rebel servant, bowing earthward
>   suppliant-wise?"
>   Abner looks, and gives him answer, "This
>   indeed is Jesse's son."
>
>   Then saith David, "Wherefore hearkenest thou, O
>   King, to words of men,
>   Saying, 'David sins against thee, and is one that
>   seeks thy hurt'?
>   When to-day I found thee sleeping like a lion in his
>   den,
>   Would I not have surely slain thee, when I cut
>   away thy skirt?
>
>   "Some there were who bade me slay thee, saying,
>   'Smite him with the sword,'
>   But I looked on thee with mercy, though thy soul
>   was in my hand.
>   For I would not lift my weapon on the chosen of the
>   Lord,
>   Neither sin against my master, though he hunts
>   me through the land.
>
>   "Who is he that thou pursuest? Who is he that thou
>   wouldst slay?
>   One that hath not done thee evil, neither sinned
>   against thy laws.
>   As a sparrow in the hedgerow, or as carrion by the
>   way,
>   Such is David, son of Jesse: may Jehovah plead
>   my cause!"

Now indeed the King is shaken; o'er him grief and
    anguish sweep:
  "Lo, is this thy voice, O David, and are these thy
      words, my son?
Let my spearmen see me humbled, and the world
    behold me weep:
  It is Saul hath done the evil; thou hast been the
      righteous one.

"Surely thou shalt bear the scepter; surely thou
    shalt wear the crown;
  For the Lord shall put dominion, power and
      kinghood in thy hand.
When before thy throne of judgment all the tribes
    of men bow down,
  Swear to hold my house in mercy: blot them not
      from out the land."

And the son of Jesse answers, "As the Lord is God
    of all,
  By His name who made the mountains and whose
      fingers formed the sea,
Never shall the hand of David sin against the blood
    of Saul:
  As the Lord shall show me mercy, there is peace
      from me to thee."

So they meet, and part forever, by the salt and
    lifeless wave,
  They that once have loved each other in the far
      and happy years:
David stands with shrouded visage at the entering of
    the cave,
  While the King turns back to Gibeah in the
      forefront of his spears.

ABIGAIL

  Saul returns from hunting; but his heart is hot
    within:
   Vain remorse and frustrate vengeance spread a
    shadow o'er his path,
  And his mind is torn with anguish and his soul is
    black with sin—
   For the King hath dealt in mercy, where he
    thought to deal in wrath.

  Saul is bowed of head and spirit, and he groans and
    grinds his teeth.
   Better to have died in battle, leaving an
    untarnished name—
  Better that the sword of David in his heart had
    found a sheath
   Than to live by David's mercy, let his spearmen
    see his shame.

  Saul returns from hunting: he hath called his
    hounds to heel,
   And the trumpets fall on silence, and the throb of
    drums is done.
  Northward through the blasted mountains moves
    the ebbing tide of steel:
   Falls again the ancient silence on the wilds of
    Jeshimon.

IV

But Jonathan returned again, and found
His friend beneath a gnarled and twisted oak
That hunched its crooked spine against the east,
Where those wild ridges ended in a bound
Of brine-burnt headlands, and the rude sea broke
In shaggy waves against them, like a slavering beast;

ABIGAIL

A place of desolation. Heaps of salt
Stood ghastly-pallid like the wife of Lot
Along the shore; there was the surges' moan;
The wind made batlike rustlings in a vault
Of chambered rock: drab twilight, like a blot,
Was thickening over all, and David stood alone.

His face turned northward, where, beyond the rim
Of wilderness, the walls of Gibeah stood
To memory's eyes pricked out in lines of fire—
The house that never more should welcome him,
The foaming stream, the whispering olive wood:
A lost but ever lovely kingdom of desire.

So Jonathan drew near, and laid a hand
On either rugged shoulder, and his eyes
Looked love upon his friend, but wakened there
No answering fire. It seemed while earth should stand
That here no more could wonder or surprise
Enkindle into flame the ashes of despair.

And David said, "I knew that thou wouldst come,
And longed for thee. But now that thou art here
I find no word of welcome, feel no joy.
For though I love thee well, my soul is dumb
Like theirs who fly the sword, yet see the spear
Lay waste their dwelling place, and the red flames destroy.

"Seest thou below us how this sea of death
Rolls deep above the cities of the plain
God smote with fire from heaven? Their tumbled walls
Are overwhelmed with brine, and none hath breath
To move among them, nor desire, nor pain;
No pipe is sounded there, no trump to battle calls.

ABIGAIL

"So is my soul: a place laid waste with fire,
And all the waves and billows of the Lord
Roll black above it, severing me from men
With floods of bitterness. No note of lyre
Nor shout of battle, nor the glittering sword,
Nor even thy dear love can bring me joy again."

The other said, "If God hath cast thee down,
It is that He may lift thee to a height
Beyond all power that men have dreamed or known;
To set upon thine head a deathless crown,
To gird thee with illimitable might,
And to assure to thee an everlasting throne.

"For so the Prophet Samuel revealed
To those around him, ere the pallid ghost
Departed from its crumbling house of clay—
That thou, and those who spring from thee, shall wield
The scepter unto Israel's utmost coast
Until the sun grow dim, the moon and stars decay."

But David said, "If this indeed be so,
What profit doth it bring, or what reward
Is in mine hand for these unfruitful years?
The seasons pass, the fire of youth burns low,
And still the heavy fingers of the Lord
Are laid upon my heart, to crush it dry of tears.

"Yet tell me—and I shame to ask, but life
Hath pressed me sore, and honor proved a wraith
No stronger than a web of gossamer—
Swear then by God: how fares it with my wife
The gentle Michal? Doth she yet keep faith?
Hath she been true to me, as I am true to her?"

ABIGAIL

Then Jonathan drew back a little space,
And bowed his face, and sharply caught his breath;
And David marked the grief unspeakable
That shook his frame. "I read it in thy face:
Yea, these are tidings bitterer than death.
I deemed her true as God; and she is false as Hell.

"Why then, let men engender with the brute!
Tear down the altar, overthrow the shrine,
Fling vows and mummery in the jackal's den!
If fairest blossoms bear such rotten fruit,
Let faith be false, and be this life of mine
A whip of scorpions to lash the lies of men!"

The Prince essayed to speak, but found no word,
And David stayed him, saying, "Speak no more.
Add not new anguish unto my despair,
Nor be thy hand the one to twist the sword
That hath already pierced me to the core.
I have enough of griefs: what is there left to bear?

"Yet go, my Prince, for thou art like a dove
That nests with vultures: thou art true alone
Among thy kindred. All I held most true
And most revered, on whom I set my love,
They have betrayed me, and are faithless grown.
Depart, lest I shall find that thou art faithless too."

So Jonathan departed, nevermore
To look on David till the day he died;
And with his going night shut down her wing
Upon the bitter sea: the dreary shore
Was blotted out, and the wild mountainside;
And in the heart of David pain alone was king.

ABIGAIL

How changeful is the heart! A bough that grief
Strips wintry bare of blossom and of bud
And leaves the shrunken twigs and wrinkled bark
As bleak as death: anon comes springing leaf,
And May returns with blossoms red as blood,
And song of nightingales amid the scented dark.

So fares man's heart: it sorrows for a while;
Yet even in its sorrow doth it learn
To list the far-off rumor of the Spring
With wind among new grasses, and will smile,
Though wanly, to behold the flowers return
To their forsaken fields, and hear the sparrow sing.

So David grieved for Michal; yet began
To smile while yet he mourned; through bleak despair
To hope against his will; the wintry blood
Ran warmer in his veins: he was a man,
No more, no less; and other forms were fair,
And other lips were sweet—and youth was yet in flood.

His grief was not as theirs who mourn their dead:
His wife had mocked him and betrayed his trust—
Or so he deemed: there was the gnawing pain
Of faith turned false, to make his lonely bed
More lonely, and his meat as bitter dust,
Till night and day alike were wormwood in his brain.

And in such mood he met with Abigail
The wife of Nabal. She was warm and quick
With bounteous life of ripened womanhood,
Fair-faced and wise. And David, through his mail,
Felt her round beauty like a dagger prick
To touch him to the heart and warm his frigid blood.

ABIGAIL

For this was in the days of shearing sheep:
The drone of bees was in the meadow flowers,
And call of birds in thicket and in grove;
Beside the threshing-floors the pipes would keep
Their teasing melody through moonlit hours,
And there was dance and song to lift the breast with love.

And thus their meeting came: for he had sent
To Nabal, saying, "Peace to thee and thine!
We kept thy shepherds safely in our land,
Nor did them hurt, but guarded flock and tent.
As God hath prospered thee with flesh and wine,
So give a blessing now into thy servant's hand."

Then Nabal answered from a churlish heart,
"Who is the son of Jesse? Yea, and whence
Is David? Many servants break their yokes
And roam as vagabonds. Shall I impart
My flesh and bread to beggars? Get ye hence,
Before I call my churls to urge your pace with strokes."

So David's envoys brought him Nabal's word:
And David answered, "Surely all in vain
Have Nabal's flocks been precious in our sight:
In vain we showed him kindness. Therefore gird
Your weapons on; for nothing shall remain
Of Nabal's, man or beast, against the morning light."

But Nabal's men told Abigail; and swift
She sped to meet the outlaws, and beseech
Their mercy on her household, turn the red
Revenge aside: with many a goodly gift
She went, and while she rode rehearsed her speech:
So met the outlaw band, and David at their head.

ABIGAIL

She lighted from her ass, and at his feet
Bowed earthward, proffering gifts of parchèd grain,
Brown loaves, red wine, and curds as white as fleece.
And David, seeing her cool and ripe and sweet,
Felt the red wrath ebb slowly from his brain,
And spake her kindly words, and bade her go in peace.

They parted then, and went their several ways,
She to her husband, David to his hold.
Yet still her voice, her gentleness, her ripe
Sweet beauty flung a glamour on his days:
Her face against the dark a lamp of gold,
Her voice in all the winds a shepherd's plaintive pipe.

So, half in love with her he left behind
At Gibeah, and half with her who bore
The name of Abigail, his lonely life
Was twice perplexed, nor any peace could find:
For one was his, yet now was his no more,
And one not his at all, but was another's wife.

And David struggled in a double mesh
Of hopeless longing, torment blent with bliss.
Two moons were his, and both were in eclipse:
He dreamt of Michal's soft and yielding flesh
Clasped in his arms, and wakened with the kiss
Of Abigail like dew upon his thirsting lips.

Then tidings reached the hold of Nabal's death
(For he had sickened from the hour he heard
How David came to smite him with his power,
With sickening fears), and this was like a breath
Of vernal wind, with twitterings of the bird,
That bids the frosted sod break forth with grass and flower.

ABIGAIL

And David sent to Abigail, and said,
"If thou wilt wed me, seeing thou art free
From Nabal, thou shalt bless an exile's life."
Then Abigail arose, and bowed her head
With joy, and said, "His servant will I be,"
And went to David's cave, and there became his wife.

V

But Michal yet was prisoner to despair.
Her days stretched black before and gray behind,
With Phaltiel's lecherous touch upon her hair,
His kisses on her mouth. The bitter rind
Of life was hers to eat; and slaves that grind
In dungeons have no greater griefs to bear.

Her flesh was his: her spirit, like a lark
That scapes the fowler's net, yet clomb the sky
And knew the sun and cloud; she there could hark
Her lover's voice, and feel his spirit nigh.
She dreamed that David's love could never die,
And David was her torch against the dark.

And Phaltiel read her fancies through his small
And crafty eyes, and was but half content
With what he saw: he held the outer wall;
The citadel withstood him. But he blent
No harshness with his kindness, came and went
With smiles, and trusted time to give him all.

His kindness made her loathe him but the more.
She did his will, too haughty to resist
Where struggling were but vanity: she wore
The guise of wife; yet ever when they kissed
Her lips were colder than the Winter mist,
Or a dead maid's, flung drowned upon the shore.

ABIGAIL

But in her secret olive wood of dream
She walked alone, for David came not now
As he had come of old: no more the beam
Of sunlight shone upon his ruddy brow;
The birds sang not; a blight was on the bough;
The flowers languished by a dying stream.

She knew not why. Could love indeed be brief?
Could vows be false, though sworn in Love's high name?
Beyond her grief could there be deeper grief—
And anguish heaped on anguish, that should maim
The soul, and make of faith a guttering flame
And life a worm upon a blasted leaf?

Ah God, was this the end? Was this the end?
The end of all, the bitter end of all?
Let darkness close around, and anguish rend
Her flesh and soul apart. Let beauty fall
In dust and desolation, like a wall
That falls in ruin labor cannot mend!

Or were her dreams but false and faithless posts
The lords of Doubt had sent her doubting mind
To scare her sleep away with fleshless ghosts
And shapes of horror, deaf and dumb and blind,
Like shapes of sand that fly before the wind
When rainless tempests shake the desert coasts?

And once she sat, upon a Summer day,
And watched the high clouds pass like drifting ships
Through heaven. Untouched her lute beside her lay;
Her breathing came and went through parted lips,
And o'er the strings were poised her fingertips
Like carven shells, as if about to play.

ABIGAIL

She was remembering a little song
Her love was wont to sing to her of old,
Before his exile and her bitter wrong
Had dimmed the dawn and marred the evening gold,
In those far days and fair; a song that told
How faith was deathless and how love was strong:

> Sweet, sweet is love, when life is at the bloom,
> Bright as a star that shines through evening gloom:
>   So shall my love ever be.
> Give all for love; yea, barter all thou hast.
> Give all for love, for only love will last.
> Love lives forever: see thou hold it fast.
>   Such is my love to thee.
>
> Fairer is love than blossoms after rain;
> Love is a moon that doth not wax nor wane:
>   So shall my love ever be.
> Love giveth all, for love will not deny.
> Love keepeth faith, and love can never lie.
> Love is of God, and so it cannot die.
>   Such is my love to thee.
>
> Love is a tree beside a flowing stream;
> Love is a waking: life is but a dream:
>   So shall my love ever be.
> Love cannot fail, whatever may betide.
> Love is immortal: it will still abide.
> May my right hand be withered at my side
>   If I be false to thee.

She mused upon the song, remembering
Those happy, happy days when life was new
And splendid, and when love alone was king.
O shameful doubts! Her David still was true
And constant as the sun to heaven. She drew
A quivering sigh, and plucked the lute to sing.

ABIGAIL

But even as she touched the strings, the door
Swung softly back, and Phaltiel came and stood
Beside her, smoothly smiling: "Love, restore
Thy smiles again, for here are tidings good:
Thy David hath consoled his widowhood;
Grieve not for him, for he is wed once more."

She stared upon him, deeming it a lie;
Yet even as she looked, in some uncouth
Embarrassment, the shifting of an eye
So schooled to fraud it wavered at the truth,
The fact stood stark before her; and the tooth
Sunk in her lips could scarce hold back a cry.

She answered not, but through her went a wail
Of anguish, though unuttered, and the blood
Froze slowly at her heart. He fixed his pale
And narrow eyes upon her face, and stood
A space in silence, smiling at her mood
In chill disdain, and then resumed his tale:

"Thy lord hath wed a dove that flocked with crows—
The widow of a vile and sottish shrew
Who stank of dung and tallow: one of those
That kennel with their beasts. The sod was new
Upon his grave, when David came to woo,
And from the dunghill plucked this perfect rose.

"For fair she is, unless my gossips be
But faithless prophets, selling lies for hire.
Fair let her be! I cavil not that he
Hath warmed his heart before another fire,
Since thou art mine. All sweetness of desire
Be his in her, like that I have in thee!"

ABIGAIL

So Phaltiel mocking spake; and Michal bowed
Her heart, but not her head. Although she heard
The crash of falling cities, and the loud
Lament of luckless captives, she must gird
Her soul with adamant. She spake no word,
But rose and sought her chamber, white and proud.

It was the end indeed: the scroll was penned
In blood and gall. Yet still must life go on.
If but the soul could into dust descend
When violets cease and nightingales are gone;
If night could tread upon the skirts of dawn,
The spirit die when hope and love have end!

She moved about her chambers, proud and pale,
And spun and sewed the seam and made the bread
Among her maidens, while she strove to veil
The darkness of her heart. And still her bed
Was mocked with dreams of David's tousled head
Pillowed upon the breast of Abigail.

Ziklag

I

Ziklag sits by the desert's edge
  In a land of ruin and sand and thorn:
Her walls are battered by Amalek's sledge;
  The horsemen of Geshur have trodden her corn.
Her palaces are a court for owls,
  Her gates are broken and burnt with flame,
Under her walls the jackal howls,
  And Ziklag the mighty is only a name.

She once was rich with wine and milk,
  With melon-gardens and citron-groves,
And the merchants came with their dates and silk,
  Almug, ivory, myrrh and cloves.
But the turbaned raiders have scourged the land
  And harrowed the fields with bloody shares:
Her wells are stopped, and the drifted sand
  Chokes and hushes her thoroughfares.

Ziklag stands at the end of the earth:
  The desert's leagues lie bare to the south,
A land of barren and bitter dearth,
  Bitten with hunger and parched with drouth.
Her gates stand wide to the hot winds' sweep;
  In courts that have heard the sentinel's tread
The lion blinks, and the lizards sleep,
  And none are there but the fleshless dead.

ZIKLAG

The last outpost of the Philistines
 To bar the way of the desert clans—
Amalek's camels have eaten her vines;
 Her walls have stabled the caravans.
And the tribesmen come and the tribesmen go,
 With turbans white as the whispering sand;
And the jackals howl, and the hot winds blow
 For ever and ever over the land.

Ziklag waits on the desert's rim,
 In a land of thirst and of thorn-trees brown;
The bones of her dead lie bleached and grim
 Where the swords of the desert have stricken them down.
And the palms' dry leaves, in the wind's hot breath,
 Rattle and clash like the strokes of brands;
And here in the fire-gnawed gateway, Death
 Sits and stares at the sunburnt sands.

Such was the place when David came,
 With crumbling breaches that gaped and grinned:
The sun above was a torch aflame,
 A scourge of steel was the desert wind.
The jackal howled and the lion roared,
 The heaven was hot as a smouldering brand;
And the lizards slept, where the desert floored
 Court and chamber with drifted sand.

II

King Saul had put aside
Ahinoam his Queen to wed another bride,
Pomegranate-lipped and swarthy: Rizpah, Aiah's child,
Who kept her father's flocks and dwelt amid the wild
Beyond Tekoa, where the brine-wet winds, that drove
The sea-born clouds before, clothed vine and olive grove
With never-withering verdure, kept the grass alive
And fresh through Summer's heat, and made each cleft a hive

ZIKLAG

Of honey-gathering bees. This region was her home—
A land of pleasant grass, grape, olive, honeycomb,
And wandering flocks of sheep and goats; but men were few—
Rough shepherds like her father, such were all she knew.
And she had grown a wild thing, shouting to her flocks
With voice of man-like strength, and laboring like an ox.
And if she had her dreams, they were of men she knew:
That Hur might smile upon her, Perez come to woo,
Or Ira wed and bear her home. The court of Saul
Was far away, nor came into her thoughts at all;
For these were but of shepherds.

                            Then, one close of day,
When sheep were in the fold, and twilight's mantle lay
Along the wrinkled hills, and like a brooch of gold
Upon a beggar's cloak, that gives its dusty fold
A regal dignity, there shone the evening star
Pale in the western sky, she took her water jar
And went to draw. For near her home there was a well
Beneath an ancient olive tree, where berries fell
And made a musty fragrance. Past the spot there ran
A road, not often trodden by the feet of man;
But hooves of goat and sheep,
Brought here for watering, had worn the earth to deep
And silent softness, so that on that dusty ground
The caravans of earth might pass without a sound.
Bending above the well to draw, she did not hear
The tread of Saul and his three thousand men draw near,
Returning from their hunt for David through the South;
But, as she straightened, Saul beheld her, and her mouth
Was like a scarlet petal of pomegranate bloom;
Her face, unveiled, seemed fair beneath the olive's gloom,
Her eyes shot back the beam
Of the lone evening star. As one that hath a dream
That lingers into waking, so the King stood still
And gazed upon the maid, while memory had her will

ZIKLAG

With him—that memory so often put aside
Because it held but pain: a damsel, starry-eyed,
Who stood beneath a darkening olive, in the glow
Of evening, in another land; how long, how long ago!

Was this not Atarah, whom he had loved so long?
He knew the thought was mad; yet like remembered song,
Or mirth in time of sorrow, when the bitter mind
Yearns for the happier past and days when life was kind,
So yearned the soul of Saul that this indeed might be
His well beloved; and the dusky olive tree
Moved gently in the wind, while through the gloom he heard
The vesper twitter of a twilight-hidden bird:
"Atarah, Atarah, Atarah!" Oh, most fair,
Loved, lost, but still remembered! Blossoms filled the air
With fragrance— Were there blossoms in this place,
Or were they madness too? Intent upon her face
He drew more near, as one bemused. And even now,
Despite his grizzled beard, gaunt cheek and furrowed brow,
Few men in Israel were goodlier than he
In face or bearing; and she saw the majesty
That marked him from his men, and knew him for the King.

The bird had hid his head beneath a drowsy wing;
The shadow and the quiet deepened, while the blood
Stood still in Rizpah's veins. Like images they stood
And stared on one another, breathless both; and twice
The King's lips moved, but spake not. With a hand like ice
He touched her face; then, like the plucked string of a harp,
The tension of his madness brake, and with a sharp
And bitter cry he turned, and muffled up his face
To hide his grief; so left her standing in her place,
And went his way toward Gibeah, followed by his band,
While she looked after him, her pitcher in her hand.

The King returned to Gibeah; yet still the ache
Was in his heart, and many a night he lay awake

ZIKLAG

Beside his wife's slow breathing, listening hour by hour
To hear the trumpet sounded from the watchman's tower,
And tossed upon his bed, while days long gone revealed
Their gilded dreams: a path across a sunburnt field,
A clump of darkening olives, and beneath their shade
A slender maid
Whose eyes looked once in his, before she drew
The veil across her face; and heaven shone with new
And splendid stars. Ah then, the days that should have been,
The days that were but dream, with Atarah his Queen,
The mother of his children, sleeping by his side
Through long, sweet nights in desert places, while the wide
Star-jeweled firmament rolled by; with her to share
His fortunes good or ill, until she saw him wear
The purple and the gold! Yea, these had been his hopes,
That died before they flowered, like grass on stony slopes
That fills no mower's hand: the lowing cattle pass
In search of greener pastures; even the wild ass
Will rather feed on thorns. And he was growing old,
With none to pity him because his heart was cold,
Or triumph in his victories, or know defeat
When he was vanquished. Those who ate his bread and meat—
This hag that shared his bed, cold-breasted, wrinkle-faced,
That bore him thankless sons, whom once he had embraced
With something like to love— He loathed her very breath
That came and went so softly! Would she mourn his death?
Or would his children? They despised him, for the sake
Of David, his supplanter. By Heaven, he would break
All teeth that gnashed at him! And Jonathan should beat
His breast in anguish; yea, and crawl, and kiss the feet
Of one he held in scorn! Ahinoam would he thrust
Aside, un-queen her, make her sit in rags and dust,
And wed another wife to spite her! He would make
His sons and daughters cringe before her! He would take
That girl with the pomegranate lips, that buxom jade
That he had come upon beneath the olive's shade

In wild Tekoa. They should all bow down their mean
And disobedient heads, and own her Israel's Queen!

And then the King would sleep, and waken with his mind
Intent on wedding Rizpah. Yet he could not find
Occasion for the deed: the chains of wont and use
Like iron fetters bound him. Wanting an excuse
He let the days drift by. Ahinoam was kind,
Most wifely and obedient, yielding to his mind
In all things great or small; and though he hated her
And sought for faults, the Queen did nothing to incur
His open wrath. And as amid the desert sand
The fiery serpent hides, till some unwary hand
Draws near and feels its fangs, so masked the King his spleen,
While Winter came and went, and tender grass grew green
Upon Tekoan hills: the flocks went forth to graze,
And lambs were white as clouds, and there were magic days
For piping and for dancing, when the singing blood
Is joyous in the veins, and love unfolds its bud
In every field and pasture, and young dreams come true.
And so it fared with Rizpah: Ira came to woo,
With gifts of cheese and oil; her father gave consent,
Their troth was plighted, and thenceforth the days were spent
In solemn preparations. So the time went by
In happiness and hope, while that high day drew nigh.

And still Ahinoam attended on her lord
With wifely gentleness, prepared his meat, and poured
His cup of wine, and strove to sooth his somber moods.
But all the days were dark, as when the tempest broods
Before it breaks in thunder; for the King's eyes burned
With ever-smouldering madness, while his household learned
To hold their breath in fear. No more the Queen could sleep
In quietness and peace; and, since her grief was deep,
She lost her self-command. And as a bow of steel
Will break when overdrawn too far, her very zeal

ZIKLAG

To keep the peace unbroken, give offense in naught,
Kept always in her thought
Forbidden things; with thinking, "I must never name
The name of Jesse's son," unwittingly it came
Upon her tongue. For Saul was raging at a raid
Against the coasts of Gad by Moab's warriors made,
Whereon the Queen cried out, "They durst not be so bold
When David kept our gates—" Then felt her heart grow cold,
And held her peace. But at the name his anger burst
In frenzy on her head: "Thou hag, of God accursed!
Spy, traitress, false and faithless! Thou and Jonathan
Thy rebel son have given allegiance to the man
Who plots against my crown!
     And darest thou name his name
In presence of thy King, and blazon forth thy shame
Before my very face? I will abide no more
Thy treacheries in my house, and from this hour my door
I bar against thee. I divorce thee from my bed
And banish thee. Thou shalt no longer eat my bread
Nor wear my raiment. By the name of God, I swear
I have endured enough. No longer will I bear
Thy hateful presence. Go!" And then, because he feared
That she might justify herself, he gnawed his beard
And lips, until his face was flecked with bloody froth,
And rolled his bloodshot eyes, not less in craft than wrath,
And tore his garments from him, while he roared and cursed,
Until Ahinoam, whose heart was like to burst
With outrage, grief and terror, stealing from the place,
Found Jonathan her son, and told him her disgrace,
And sobbed, and cried "Alas!" until her voice grew dumb
From very agony. And the Prince bade her come
To his own house and rest, while he would see the King
And make her peace; and she should take it as a thing
Of little moment, knowing how his father's mind
Was vexed with evil spirits. Yet he still was kind,
And would repent his words.

ZIKLAG

      But when he went to speak
With Saul, he found his eyes like embers in his cheek
That flamed at sight of him, and a malignant grin
Curled back his lips to show the snarling teeth within,
Yet slimed with blood and foam. For Saul had conjured up
His demon to his aid, and it had held the cup
Of fury to his lips: the King had drunk the broth
Brewed in the Devil's cauldron, till his heart was wroth
Beyond all governance. The Prince stood still, amazed,
Nor spake, while on his head his father's anger blazed:
"Dog! Traitor! David's vassal! Darest thou draw nigh
Unbidden to the King? By Him that rules on high
As I do reign on earth, thou mightest safelier tread
The dragon's fiery den. Thy blood be on thy head."
Thereon he raised his javelin; but the Prince drew near
Until he felt the spear
Prick at his ribs, and answered, "Seeing thou hast slain
My spirit, should I care that flesh and bones remain
To walk an empty earth? Yet hold a space, and hear
The word I have to speak; and after, let thy spear
Strike through mine entrails. Thou hast sent to banishment
The man that most I loved, though he was innocent
Of wrong against thee. Thou my sister hast defiled
With an adulterous marriage. Me hast thou exiled,
And twice hast sought to slay me. Last, and most debased,
Beyond all infamies of men, thou hast disgraced
Ahinoam my mother—her who blessed thy youth
With faithfulness and service—given her to the tooth
Of slander in her age. O Saul, I am thy son
And may not curse thee; but God marks what thou hast done,
And shall not He requite it?"

      Not since Samuel died
Had any in the kingdom dared Saul's towering pride,
Or answered him again. As one that in a dream
Chastises some poor bondman, who can only scream

ZIKLAG

And cringe and plead for mercy—then a shade like death
Falls sudden o'er the vision, and within a breath
His victim's form is changed to one of giant size
That towers high above him, with unpitying eyes,
With dreadful weapons girded, panoplied in mail—
So feels his blood run cold, his countenance grow pale,
And wakens mute with terror; thus it was with Saul:
He felt a darkness fall
Across his soul, and in it cities flamed, and spears
Flashed forth like lightnings; there were trumpets in his ears,
And walls went tumbling down in ruin. Then there thronged
Around him haggard shapes of all that he had wronged,
Oppressed and done to death: the Prophet Samuel came
With sad, reproachful visage; Michal, bowed in shame,
And David, with the fringe. Ahinoam was there
With patient, piteous eyes; Ahimelech's hoary hair
Befouled with dirt and blood; and many more beside
That he had wronged and ruined. Mute and hollow-eyed
They stood and looked upon him: on his gilded throne
He writhed like one in torment; with a face of stone
He looked on Jonathan, and answered, "I am he
Who ruins all he touches. This is God's decree,
And who can stand against it? There was one of old
Who found no place of penitence, because he sold
His right of birth to feed his hunger. I have sinned
Like him beyond all penitence, and every wind
Brings doom and desolation. I am like to one
Dragged at the chariot's wheel behind his foe. My son,
Console thy mother's heart, and wipe away her tears.
My time is hard at hand: a cry is in my ears,
The shout of the avenger. When the curse shall fall
Upon my head in thunders, and the soul of Saul
Goes to its bitter end, Jehovah grant to thee
The mercy and the peace that are denied to me."
He ceased, and bowed his head; and with a bitter groan
The Prince stole from the place, and left the King alone.

ZIKLAG

But Saul was still intent
On wedding Rizpah; and he tarried not, but sent
Doeg the Edomite, and bade him find the girl
And fetch her back to him. And thereupon the churl
Took men and beasts and went, and reached the wilderness
Beyond Tekoa, now arrayed in vernal dress,
And white with straying flocks, and loud with droning bees,
Yellow with grain, and gray with silvery olive trees,
But scant of folk, save shepherds and rude husbandmen;
And ever as he went he asked, and asked again,
Of such a maid as Rizpah; learned she was the child
Of Aiah, and betrothed to Ira. Doeg smiled
His slow and crooked smile, and hid his mules, and lay
In wait beside the way
By which the marriage party should pass by at eventide;
And in due time there came the bridegroom and the bride,
With shepherd lads and damsels, singing as they went
The old, old marriage songs. His sudden onslaught sent
The revelers flying; but he seized upon the maid,
Bedecked with rustic ornaments, and all arrayed
To please her husband's eyes: they got their mules, and sped
Toward Gibeah of Saul, while Ira gathered head
To follow after them.
     And Saul, in shameful haste,
His household summoned to the marriage, and embraced
The buxom Rizpah (while gray-haired Ahinoam
Sorrowed in exile), calling her his little lamb,
His star-eyed dove, his Atarah, lost so long,
But loved and still desired, his music and his song.
And all the while, clasped in the gray King's arms, she yearned
For far Tekoan pastures, and her heart returned
To Ira, strong and young, her well-loved shepherd groom:
So lost her eyes their light, her lips their scarlet bloom,
And she repined and sickened, flinching from the scorn
Of those about the court who deemed her meanly born,

ZIKLAG

Nor fit to wed the King. Then Saul, who heard her name
Her Ira's name in secret reverie, felt a flame
Flash through his blood, and fumed all day, and at the last
Sent Doeg, bidding him to slay the man, and cast
His carcase on the dunghill. And the Edomite,
Who loved iniquity as better men love right,
Went forth in haste.

     But Ira, being warned, had fled,
And came to David's hold with ashes on his head
To seek asylum. And the gentle Abigail
(Whose lord was not at home: for he had gone in mail
With nearly all his spears, to battle with a band
Of Geshurites that plundered Simeon's borderland
And robbed the threshing-floors), received the fugitive,
And bade him stay until her lord should come, and give
His sentence in the matter. So the shepherd tarried
And ate of David's bread, while Doeg's spearmen harried
Tekoa's Wilderness, and slaughtered peaceful folk,
And reddened earth with fire and dimmed the sky with
  smoke;
For such was Saul's revenge.

     And on the second day
They came to David's hold. There was the sudden bray
Of ram's horn, clang of sword on helmet, and the thrust
Of spear on sounding shield: blood dripped upon the dust,
And there was chance and skill, wounds, death; and over all
The shout of Doeg: "Slay the rebels! Strike for Saul!"
But few the outlaws were, and bitterly bestead
By overwhelming numbers, armed from heel to head;
Yet long and well they strove, and still before the cave
A dwindling handful battled; Ira, with a glaive,
Withstood the Edomite, who, armored in cuirass
Of bull-hide leaved with bronze, steel helm and greaves of
  brass,
Was like a tower of stone.

ZIKLAG

                But, from his petty war
Returning home victorious, David heard afar
The ram's horn blown, the din, the shout, the stroke of blade
On brazen helm and bull-hide buckler furious laid,
And winged his feet to fiery speed, and reached the scene
Before the fight was lost. He flung himself between
Ira and Doeg, there, and with a single thrust
Of that skilled spear he rolled the Edomite in dust,
Wide-sprawled and scant of breath. Before the man could rise
His sword was out of sheath, and bit between the eyes,
And clave the casque in twain, and split the skull-bone wide,
Scattering the brains upon the ground. In such wise died
Doeg the Edomite. With that came up the rest
Of David's followers, like hornets when their nest
Is shaken. Breaking forth in wild and clamorous shout,
They dealt unstinted blows, till onset turned to rout,
And Doeg's spearmen fled, and came to Gibeah's wall
With tidings for the King that filled his heart with gall.

III

Then David reasoned in his heart, and said,
"The chance will surely change, and I shall die
By Saul's contrivance, saving that I fly
To Achish, King of Gath, and put my head
In his protection. For I well may find
More mercy with the heathen than with him
That rules in Israel, and hath set his mind
Upon my death. Beyond Philistia's rim
Saul cannot reach, and surely will despair
Of me; and I shall be in safety there."

He summoned of his band the head and chief
To parley, saying how greatly had advanced
Their danger, through this battle that had chanced
And Doeg's death, and spake of his belief

ZIKLAG

That they must quit the land, and sell their swords
And services in warfare unto those
Who ruled along the coast, Philistia's lords,
And find protection with their country's foes,
Rather than tarry longer where the power
Of Saul should be their peril every hour.

Then Eleazar straight approved the scheme,
But Abishai was all for tarrying
To match their might in warfare with the King
And seek to break his power; and Jashobeam
Inquired, "What welcome shall we find in Gath?
Have they forgot so soon it was thy stone
That slew their champion? Will they not in wrath
Arise and rend our bodies flesh from bone?
So should we be like one that flees a bear,
And puts his head into the lion's lair."

And David answered, laughing in his beard,
"Whoever talked in David's camp before
Of safety? We have heard the thunderous roar
Where iron-ribbed War stands helmeted and speared—
And speak we now of safety? Who is safe
But he that fears no terror? But the law
Hath bound our hands: however much he chafe
Against us in his wrath, we may not draw
Against the King. And yet, it suits not men
To die like vermin smothered in their den.

"As for the Lord of Gath: although I brake
Goliath's skull, and wear his sword in sheath,
I trow that Achish did not mourn his death,
And will not much mislike me for his sake.
Yea, rather he will prize me, that I killed
The man that most he feared, and saved his throne
From one that hated him, and thought to build
A kingdom on the ruin of his own.

ZIKLAG

This Achish will befriend us if he can,
And all Philistia's nobles fear the man."

Then Joab answered, saying, "Who shall stand
Against the will of David? God most high
Hath been his helper, and He yet is nigh
To bless the son of Jesse. Thy command,
O David, will we keep; and thine we are
To do thee service and obey thy word,
To trust thee unto death in peace or war,
To follow thee in exile, or to gird
Our swords behind thee, till the Lord shall bring
Thy foes to kiss thy feet, and make thee King."

The rest agreed; and having stripped the slain
That lay about the cave of arms and mail,
They set upon their journey; crossed the Vale
Of Sorek, and advanced across the plain
Toward Gath. And seeing them, the reapers flung
Their sickles down, and fled in hot retreat
For safety, while the trumps with brazen tongue
Blared the alarm, and drums began to beat,
And from the city issued an array
Of chariots and men to bar their way.

But David sent an embassy to hold
A parle with Achish, since they came as friends,
To do him service, and to make amends
For harms that they had caused his realm of old;
They had escaped from Saul, whose bloody hand
Was stretched to slay them, and they sought a place
Of peace and refuge in Philistia's Land:
Would Achish deign to look upon the face
Of David and his men, and give them room
To dwell in Gath, and save them from their doom?

ZIKLAG

So Achish welcomed them; and so they dwelt
At Gath, that strange, rich city of the plain,
Engirt with vineyard lands and fields of grain
And olive-dowered hills. And Achish dealt
With them in kindliness. And when the lords
Protested, and the nobles of the realm,
That he had harbored Israelitish swords
To rend Philistia's shield and dint her helm,
He answered, "Saul hath flung his sword away:
Shall I not gird it for the battle day?"

Now David, passing to his lodgings, saw
A withered crone, appareled in the guise
Of Israel's women. Listless were her eyes
And dead to hope; her hair, like beaten straw,
Half hid the wrinkled face. She might have been
The eldest child of Time, so bowed with care
And years she was, as if her eyes had seen
All agony, all sorrow, all despair,
And all the sins that marred the face of man
And darkened earth with grief, since time began.

And David felt a shudder shake his frame,
As one who sees a beast in mortal pain,
That hath no voice to groan or to complain,
Will shudder; and a sickening pity came
Upon him, for her face held no desire,
But looked as one that lives and yet hath died,
On whom the torments of eternal fire
Have burned, yet left the soul unpurified;
Who must endure, until the Judgment Day,
Such sins as anguish cannot purge away.

So, groaning in his heart, he asked of one
Whom Achish had appointed for his guide,
"Who is the woman there, so hollow-eyed,
That watched us pass? It seemed that life had done

Its worst with her." The Philistine replied,
"The Hebrew sorceress, who sayeth sooth.
They all but slew her when she prophesied
Against the kings, although she spake the truth.
But she is crazed with torture, and her name
She hath forgot, and even whence she came."

And David, moving to his house, was mute
With pity for the woman, who had sprung
From his own race. What sorrows might her tongue
Relate; and of what black and bitter fruit
Had she not tasted? Yet he put the thought
Aside, for other cares. The gates were stout:
If war should rise, his men and he were caught
As in a lion's cage—and growing doubt
Oppressed his spirit; for he was aware
Of furtive looks, and rumors in the air.

For there abode Goliath's kindred yet
In Gath: Benesasira, Lahmi, Saph,
Of monstrous stature; each could wield for staff
A chariot's pole; and all of them had set
Their hearts on slaying David, to requite
Their kinsman's death. But knowing that his hand
Was strong to wield the sword, they nursed their spite,
And sowed the streets with whispers that he planned
To send their king a hostage to his lord,
And put the city to the torch and sword.

And in a breathless midnight, when the mouse
Squeaked in the closet, and the beetles clicked
In rotting beams, and David's eardrums pricked
With doubtful sounds, the sorceress sought his house;
And, blinking like a weasel at the light,
She plucked his garment with a bony thumb
And finger, mumbling with gray lips, "The night
Is filled with terrors, and thy doom is come.

ZIKLAG

Dost thou not hear the giants, as they whet
Their swords, to pay thee back their bloody debt?

"I am a poor old woman, and I dream.
But I can see through walls that have no chink,
And hear the secret things the nobles think,
Although they hide in closets— Never deem
I have no soul. They lie! It hath a sting
That strikes me like a scorpion, and my wit
Is numbed with pain. I cannot wed the King,
Because my sister robbed me—" Here a fit
Of cackling laughter seized her, high and shrill
As early cock-crow on a far-off hill.

And David answered, "Tarry here and rest.
My wife will shelter thee, and ease thy heart
With gentleness: for old and sad thou art,
And pitiful. But I will make request
For thee of Achish. Thou hast come to warn
A stranger of his peril: recompense
Shall be repaid thee. Achish will not scorn
To grant my boon; and I will take thee hence
And keep thee safe." But while he spake, the same
Unmirthful laughter shook her withered frame.

So Abigail received her, and with kind
And soothing words entreated her, and pressed
Her bony hands, beseeching her to rest
In her own chamber, praying she might find
Both peace and comfort; till she ceased her wild
And cackling laughter, and began to weep
In sobs and gasping murmurs, like a child
Whose mother comforts her; and fell asleep,
To dream of windy olives, and the smell
Of ripening grapes, before she passed through Hell.

ZIKLAG

At morning, David sought the King, and said,
"My Lord, if we find favor in thine eyes,
I pray thee give to us some place that lies
Beyond thy walls: for wherefore should we tread
The royal city? Grant me some frontier
To guard for thee, that I may prove my hate
Of them that hate thee, with my sword and spear,
And I will be the guardian of thy gate."
And Achish answered, "Therefore be it known
That I do give thee Ziklag for thine own."

Then David answered, "Let my master hear
His servant further. Thou dost captive hold
A Hebrew woman: she is weak and old,
Worthless to thee; but Israel's speech is dear
Unto her heart. I pray thee then, bestow
Thy prisoner on thy servant; and my sword
Shall serve thee well therefor, and thou shalt know,
For this thy mercy, mercy from the Lord."
And Achish answered, "Freely I resign
To thee this sorceress: she is also thine."

IV

Then David straightway armed his band
And southward marched across the land,
To where, upon the desert's rim,
Lay Ziklag, ruinous and grim,
With battered walls, untenanted
By any but the fleshless dead.

In sooth, the place was chosen well
For hard-faced sons of war to dwell;
For though to northward there were clumps
Of scraggly fig, and olive stumps,
And fields where once had been the plough
And sickle, all was lifeless now;

ZIKLAG

And southward, far as eye could see,
Stretched the waste sand's immensity,
Now bare as death itself, now white
With turbans of the Geshurite
Or Amalek's sons; and war of old
Had wasted wine-press, lodge and fold,
Had stopped the wells with sand and stones,
And left but heaps of whitening bones
That once were men. There was no sound
But lizards skittering o'er the ground,
And winds that ever scoured the land,
Hot from the leagues of blinding sand.

But David filled the breaches wide
With fallen stones, refortified
The broken gates, and built once more
The sagging roof and mouldered door,
Unstopped the spring and cleared the well,
And made a place where men could dwell.

So Ziklag, city of the dead,
Was once again inhabited,
And warriors laid aside their shields
To drive the share through stony fields,
While women baked and wove and spun,
And pipes were played when day was done.
And there they built, of stone and clod,
An altar unto Israel's God,
Whereon Abiathar the Priest
Poured out the blood and burned the beast.

But, though they turned to peaceful toil,
And dressed the vine and tilled the soil,
The sturdy arts of war were yet
Remembered: still the watch was set
Upon the ramparts; spear and brand
Were kept in order and at hand;

ZIKLAG

And plundering desert rovers learned
That sword and buckler had returned
To Ziklag's walls, to bar the path
Toward Gaza and the gates of Gath.

For twice the hosts of Amalek came
With crooked swords that flashed like flame,
And once the sun shone hot and bright
On lances of the Geshurite
Before their walls. But David's men
Beat back the threatening tide again.
Yet still his power was weak, nor might
Assail the foes in open fight.

But soon his band began to swell
With refugees from Israel;
Outlaws from Judah and the coast
Of Simeon—a growing host
That fled the fury of the King;
Stout warriors, armed with bow and sling,
Who used the right and left hands both
In shooting; and they all made oath
Of truth to David. Last of all
Came exiles of the house of Saul,
From Benjamin; and David went
To meet them, saying, "If ye be sent
As spies of Saul against my band,
And treachery be in your hand,
Then may our fathers' God condemn
Your sin. But if ye be of them
That help my cause, our hearts shall be
Close-knit with yours in amity."
And one, the leader of their band,
Made answer, "Faith is in our hand.
Thine are we, David! On thy side,
Thou son of Jesse! Peace abide

ZIKLAG

With thee, and all that hold thy rod
In reverence. It is thy God
That helpeth thee; and He shall tread
Thy foes in dust, and crown thine head."

So David's might from day to day
Waxed more and more, till he could say
With kindling eyes, "By God's high throne,
These desert raiders have not known
The strength of men! For they but war
On sheepcote and on threshing-floor!
Ye sons of Israel, gird the blade,
And let us teach these thieves the trade
Of thrust and blow!" And so one morn
The drums beat loud, the twisted horn
Proclaimed the march; and David chased
The raiders through their sandy waste.
He slaughtered Geshur in his tents
And filled the desert with laments;
He smote of Amalek's swarthy sons
To where the Brook of Egypt runs;
And so returned, with spoil of flocks,
The high-humped camel, ass, and ox.
Then they that bode at home came forth
To welcome him with dance and mirth,
And beasts were slain and wine was poured
To Israel's God, who blessed the sword.

Now there was brought among the spoil
A group of captives, bent with toil
And bondage: mowing scanty grass
Beside the brooks for ox and ass,
Worn down with beating out the grain
And lading beasts, since Saul's campaign
Against the tribes of Amalek
Had set the yoke upon their neck.

ZIKLAG

These men were brought to David now,
And did obeisance, till the brow
Scraped in the dust. And David said,
"Arise and stand. I draw no blade
Against the captive or the bond.
Whence came ye?" One replied, "Beyond
The northern mountains is our home;
The land of milk and honeycomb—
We are of Israel." David said,
"Would ye return?" They bowed the head
And wept. Then David said, "Return
Unto your land again, and learn
That God is good. And ye shall take
Food for the journey that ye make;
And for the labor ye have done,
Take of the spoil our swords have won
From them that wronged you. Ye shall keep
Each one an ass and twenty sheep;
And when ye come to Israel, bless
The Lord, who pitied your distress.

"Yet stay! I have a woman here,
Philistia's captive many a year,
So overworn by wrong and shame
She hath forgotten whence she came,
Or who she is or where she stayed,
Yet knows herself a Hebrew maid.
Take ye this woman. She is old
And poor, but I will give you gold,
And ye shall buy a plot of ground
With figs and vines, amid the sound
Of mountain winds, where she may dwell,
And hear the speech of Israel.
Where is your home?" One answered, "Far
En-dor, in northern Issachar."
And David asked, "What matter where?
Buy ye for her a garden fair,

ZIKLAG

    And let her dwell in peace, among
    The people of her race and tongue."

    The men agreed, and took their sheep
    And asses, and for each a heap
    Of food and raiment; and the gray
    And withered Atarah went her way
    With them, and gentle Abigail
    Stood in the gateway, sad and pale,
    To watch her go.

                  Then David made
    Choice of the plunder of his raid,
    Apparel, weapons, cakes of dates,
    And brought them all to Gath's high gates
    A gift to Achish, saying, "Behold,
    Thy servant David hath been bold
    Against thy foes; and now we bring
    The choicest plunder to the King."

    And Achish said, "That ye fought best
    These laden camels all attest.
    But whither hast thou made this raid?"
    And David said, "I drew my blade
    On Judah's southern coasts, and beat
    The people down beneath my feet."

    Then Achish stroked his beard, and said,
    "I make thee keeper of mine head;
    For thou this day hast stricken hard
    Against mine enemies, and marred
    The beard of Saul. Behold, the hour
    Draws near when we shall break his power;
    And ye shall go with me to war
    Against this King, whom ye abhor
    Not less than we." And David made
    Reply: "When thou shalt gird thy blade,

There let me be, with spear and shield,
Beside thee on the battlefield."

Then spake the King, "I have no son;
And when I perish, there is none
That owns my breath or blood, to wear
The crown of Gath as Achish' heir.
These giants of Goliath's clan
Are set in purpose to a man
To seize the palace and the throne
If I grow faint. Thy hand alone
Is with me: do thou valiantly
And fight my wars, and thou shalt be
The King of Gath."

    So David went
Back to his city, well content,
To listen to the camel bells,
And watch the folk about the wells,
And those long furrows that the share
Turned up, and find that life was fair.
He saw his people dwell in peace,
With roof and raiment, food and fleece,
Unharmed of turmoil or of wrath,
And dreamed himself the King of Gath.

V

Meantime, the little band of refugees
 Moved northward through the Land of Simeon,
Till mountains rolled around, like emerald seas
 That flash beneath the sun.

For now had come the time of Autumn rain,
 When pasture lands show hints of feathery green,
And brooks go singing their old, sweet refrain
 Their reedy banks between.

ZIKLAG

And slowly did they move: the sheep must graze
   Along the ways, the asses find their food;
But to the toil-bowed exiles all the days
   Were filled with peace and good.

And Atarah's eyes shone with their old, soft light,
   Like April stars above a misty plain:
This was her well-loved land; and day and night
   Brought quiet to her brain.

Faint memories stole back of things forgot
   Long since; the rushes bending with the stream,
The dew that vanished as the sun grew hot—
   All these were like a dream.

They came to Rama, where her childhood days
   Had run like ripples in a silvery tide,
And Atarah looked upon familiar ways,
   And wist not why she sighed.

For in this changeful world where all things change,
   The blood and tears of piteous days may blot
The scroll of memory. The scenes were strange:
   She looked, but knew them not.

Thus came the exile home, but came too late:
   For he who watched with piteous eyes of yore
For her returning, from the towered gate,
   Now watched for her no more.

And so they came to Gibeah of Saul,
   Where grave men trod the streets with troubled eyes.
The royal standard drooped upon the wall
   Against the darkening skies.

ZIKLAG

The city seemed a dwelling of the dead:
   Ahinoam was banished from the place,
And Jonathan, in wrath at Saul, had fled
   To share the Queen's disgrace.

And many more of valor and of worth
   Had followed him, or fled to the retreat
Of David. All was grim: there was no mirth,
   No harping in the street.

But in the cheerless palace, hollow-eyed
   And prey to grisly terrors and alarms,
A mad King fondled an unwilling bride
   And clasped her in his arms;

While through his streets there passed, as in a dream,
   The woman he had loved so long and dear,
And would have given his kingdom to redeem—
   He knew not she was near.

Yea, so return our dreams, lovely and kind,
   With hands stretched out to bless us; but the heart
Is holden by its griefs, the soul is blind;
   And sadly they depart.

So came, at last, the travelers to that place
   Where En-dor sits upon its rocky hill
Against the sky, and round its caverned base
   The winds go whistling shrill.

The captives were returned; and there were cries
   Of wonder and surprise, with honeycomb
And bread and wine set forth, and shining eyes
   To greet the exiles home.

ZIKLAG

They bought for Atarah, with David's gold,
    A plot of land, with vines and olive trees,
A little house to keep her from the cold,
    A garden, sweet with bees.

And there she dwelt alone, and dressed her vines,
    And digged her tiny garden, and she sold
Her herbs, and so forgot the Philistines
    And all her griefs of old.

Yet since she lived alone, and often spoke
    With mumbling lips when none was nigh to hear,
The children shunned her, and the village folk
    Regarded her with fear,

And called her witch, and said that she possessed
    Familiar spirits, and could prophesy,
Or call the dead from their unhallowed rest,
    And had the evil eye.

So harvest came, with corn in yellowing ear,
    And Atarah gleaned the barley of En-dor
Behind the reapers. And the time drew near
    When kings go forth to war.

Gilboa

I

ALL THINGS shall have an end: the more and less
Contrived of men, the cities and the towers
   Are overturned by the unpitying hours,
And sown with ashes of forgetfulness.

Go, seek the kingdoms that were great of yore:
   For Noph lies waste, and Nineveh forgets;
   On Tyre's wet rocks the fishers spread their nets,
And Ilium is a memory by the shore.

Yea, ask of Gibeah, or ask of Gath!
   They now are resting places for the flocks;
   The conies hide among their tumbled rocks,
And Time hath swept their glories from his path.

And Saul and Achish—names by men forgot,
   Blurred characters in some old manuscript,
   Long hid and mouldering in a sunless crypt
O'er which the shepherd treads, and dreams it not.

Their trumps are silent and their standards furled;
   Their laurels have been withered by the gust;
   Their fiery hearts are crumbled into dust
To ride the winds that blow across the world.

Yet once their shouting shook the earth with dread;
   At their command would thousands gird the sword—
   The chariots thundered and the trumpets roared,
And war's red harvest heaped the fields with dead.

GILBOA

The time returned when kings go forth to war,
   And posts went racing through Philistia's realm;
   The harness glittered, and the plume-topped helm;
And drums were loud, and beacons flamed afar,

While through her wondering cities went the cry,
   "Yoke ye the snorting coursers, mount the car,
   Brace on the buckler, bend the bow of war,
And gird the flashing sword upon the thigh!

"Ye Kings of Gaza and of Gath, arise!
   Ye Lords of Ashdod and of Ashkelon,
   Bring forth your chariots, flaming like the sun,
And let the lances gleam against the skies.

"Upon the helmet bind the nodding plume;
   Endue the habergeon, anoint the targe
   For battle; and let yawning Hell enlarge
Her borders, and the haughty dead make room!

"Make room by black Cocytus, for the sons
   Of Israel! Marna's thunderbolts are forged
   To cast them down: the ravens shall be gorged
With flesh of captains and of mighty ones."

II

Terrible brazen laughter of trumpets madly blown;
Beat of the drums of battle to turn the heart to stone;
   Muster of mail-clad forces,
   Stamp and whinny of horses,
Chariots rolling, rolling on to overturn a throne!

March of the host to battle, with standards wide unfurled,
Shout of the kings and captains in loud defiance hurled,

And the vultures fly together,
Birds of an ominous feather,
Where the terrible ones go marching up to the top
of the world.

We shall have them in derision, say the
trumpets of Philistia,
We shall have them in derision, say the drums:
We shall have them in derision, in the Valley
of Decision,
For the seers have seen the vision, and the day
of fury comes.

Up through the Plain of Sharon, yellow with
ripened grain,
The kings go forth for glory like merchantmen for
gain,
And the swords and torches redden
The passage of Armageddon,
Where the Philistines go winding down to
Esdraëlon's Plain.

Here, where the host of Jabin with iron chariots
came,
Where Sisera blew the trumpet to win himself a
name,
And the stars, in their heavenly courses,
Whelmed him, footmen and horses,
And the sword of Barak threshed them, and
Deborah sang their shame—

Here, where the rebel nations shall stand with
shield and sword,
When the trumpets of God are sounded and the
vials of wrath outpoured
(The vials and trumpets seven)
Till fire shall fall from Heaven,
And they from the earth be blotted in the dreadful
Day of the Lord—

GILBOA

Here are the legions marching, with flash and
    shimmer of spears,
The blast of the brazen trumpet and throb of the
    drumbeat nears;
  The chariots jingle and glisten,
  The reeds stand still to listen
Along the banks of the Kishon, to the shouts of the
    charioteers.

  We shall tread them down as stubble, says the
    jingling of the harness;
  We shall tread them down as stubble, flash the
    spears.
  We shall tread them down as stubble, pay them
    back in measure double,
  For their pride is but a bubble, and the day of
    vengeance nears.

Up from the plain of the Kishon, bannered and
    girded for war,
Up to the highlands of Issachar—Jezreel, Shunem,
    En-dor,
  While the mountains and valleys are shaken
  With echoes the trumpets awaken,
The host of the terrible people cometh a conqueror.

Go up to bare Gilboa; make thee a stronghold, O
    Saul!
Summon the tribes to battle with beacon and
    trumpet-call.
  For all things made have ending;
  And into the dark descending
Thou and thy realm shall perish, and darkness shall
    cover all.

GILBOA

Hark to the brazen challenge of terrible trumpets
    blown;
Hark the reverberant drumbeat, to turn thy heart
    to stone;
  The tramp of the mail-clad forces,
  The stamp and whinny of horses,
The rumble and roll of the chariot-host to
    overturn thy throne!

  We shall rend their shields asunder, scream the
    trumpets of Philistia;
  We shall rend their shields asunder, roll the
    drums.
  We shall rend their shields asunder when our
    chariots roll like thunder;
  We shall gather up the plunder, when the day
    of battle comes.

Look on their host and tremble: they fill thy wide
    domain
With a hum like the hum of locusts that cover hill
    and plain.
  And the ravens gather together,
  Birds of a sable feather;
The kites and vultures assemble to feast upon the
    slain.

Mark, and be dumb with terror. Summon the seers
    to divine,
Call for the Urim and Thummim—Jehovah, show
    us a sign!
  If the prophets can give no answers,
  Then seek for the necromancers;
Seek for the wizards that mutter, the witches that
    mumble and whine!

GILBOA

"Seek," said King Saul, "for a woman skilled in the
    sorceress' trade,
One who can summon me Samuel out of the night
    and the shade;
Let her reveal me the morrow,
    Show me its triumph or sorrow—
The prophets will give me no answer, and terrors
    have made me afraid."

Then they made answer and told him, "Wouldst
    thou be wise for the war?
Lo, there is one that can aid thee, one of the trade
    men abhor,
    Learned in incantation,
    Magic and dark divination—
One with a spirit familiar: there is a witch at
    En-dor."

III

Philistia's vanguard, under the command
Of Hanun, pitched in Shunem; and the land
Burned like an oven, where the torch of war
Laid waste the villages of Issachar,
With wail of luckless captives, and the cry
Of folk who watched the smoke-wreaths climb the sky
From house and vineyard. But the greater host
Was gathering yet at Aphek, nigh the coast,
Where Achish pitched his tent; and day by day
New-formed battalions marched upon their way
Up Carmel's rugged slope, and down again
Through Esdraëlon—chariots and men
And bows and javelins; and one could feel
The hard earth shaken with the grinding wheel
And tramp of warriors.

GILBOA

              David, tarrying still
At Aphek, waited for his master's will
To send him onward. Faithful to his word,
He willingly had followed when he heard
The summons of his lord, nor had he stayed
To seek celestial counsel, but arrayed
His band, and hastened northward to the place
Of mustering; and though sometimes the face
Of Jonathan or Michal seemed to look
Reproachfully upon him, yet he shook
The fancy from him: hardening his heart
To fight with Saul, he watched the bands depart,
Eager to follow. Yet was Achish loath
To part with David, and had sworn an oath
That he would make him guardian of his head
Forever after, and that they should tread
The fields of war together. There had grown
A bond betwixt them—something of the bone
And sinew more than of the heart: a hard
And bloodless friendship, built on that regard
Which warrior feels for warrior. Achish knew
His vassal's power in war, and gave him due
Respect and honor; David marked the keen
Thrust of his mind, and was content to lean
On Achish' judgment, as he moved his bands,
Like carven pieces that the player's hands
Deploy across the chess-board—here a pawn
Advanced a square, and here a knight withdrawn
To guard a castle—so he moved his men
Across the checkerboard of hill and glen
And plain and river, with his crafty eyes
Smiling to think a kingdom was the prize.

But David's foemen of Goliath's clan
Sowed rumors in the camp, till men began
To murmur, "Wherefore come these Hebrews here?
Are they not like to fall upon our rear

And strike for Saul their King? Behold, we know
A faithless friend is worse than open foe."
And others said that Achish, being old,
Had fallen on dotage; and the tale was told
That David had sent messengers by stealth
To Saul the King, and wished him peace and health,
Had pledged him help, and promised him the head
Of Hanun. And this rumor ever spread
Throughout Philistia's camp.

       The day was come
For march, with trumpet-blast and throb of drum:
The tents were struck in Aphek; wheel and hoof
Moved northward through Manasseh, o'er the roof
Of Carmel, and Philistia's mighty horde
Through Esdraëlon marched, and neared the ford
Of hurrying Kishon. David, in the rear,
Passed on with Achish, armed with shield and spear,
And with him all his band. But soon began
A murmur in the host: from man to man
The whisper went, "Behold, the Gittite fox
Hath lost his cunning and is mad. A pox
Upon his folly! Shall these men, the pride
Of Israel's arms, not strike upon the side
Of Israel?" So questionings and doubts
Swelled into clamorous wrath, that burst in shouts
And imprecations; there were waving swords
And clashing bucklers; and Philistia's lords,
Rusa of Gaza, and stout Adimar
Of Ashdod, reining back their steeds of war,
Inquired the cause, and hearing, gave commands
The trump should sound a halt, and all the bands
Stood still bewildered; coursers champed the bit
And pawed the earth, unwilling to submit
To quiet; and the princes turned the rein
And gave their steeds the whip, and made the plain

Smoke with their speed; so came where Achish sat
Upon his chariot, blinking like a cat
And smiling through his beard. And Achish said,
"By Dagon's fishy tail and Marna's head,
If ye but drive on Saul with half the speed
Ye waste to-day, the war is ours indeed!
What seek ye here? Your post is with your bands.
And in this place the King of Gath commands."

And Adimar replied, "Because thy hair
Is white, we pass thine insults. Must we bear
Thy follies too? What do these Hebrews here,
Armed to the foot, and marching in our rear?
If thou dost set no value on thy head,
We cherish ours, and will not make our bed
With wolves of Jacob."

     Achish said, "In sooth,
The dog is half a wolf, yet sets his tooth
In his wolf-brother, being trained of man
To war with wolves. And since these men began
To be my vassals, faithful have they been
In all their dealings. I have found no sin
In David or his men. For these are they
Who served with Saul; and yet they fell away
And joined our cause. They eat my bread and salt
And serve me truly. I have found no fault
In David's hand."

     And Rusa said, "Belike
Ye find no hurt in serpents till they strike.
But then the venom, spreading through the veins,
Sets all the blood afire with mortal pains
And stills the heart; and so too late ye learn
Your folly. Therefore bid these men return
To their appointed city, lest in guile
They strike us in the back, and reconcile

Their master with our heads. For this is he
Of whom their women sang in minstrelsy,
'Saul slew his thousands: Jesse's son hath slain
His tens of thousands.' And if these remain
They are a peril to us and a snare,
And weaken every arm. We will not bear
The risk, O King of Gath: thou goest too far
Beyond authority."

    Then Adimar
Made answer, "By our mother Derketo,
The Queen of Heaven, except thou bid them go,
We do renounce the war, and will recall
Our vassals, leaving thee to deal with Saul
Alone; for Hanun also will return
And leave the war to thee, if thou shalt spurn
Our counsel."

    Then said Gaza's King, "Advise
Thy stubborn heart. Since men account thee wise,
Give not the lie to thy renown, but yield
To our demands, before we quit the field,
And these bright banners—Ekron's dolphin flag,
And Ashdod's eagle and thy running stag,
Mine own proud ensign decked with moon and sun
And the red pelican of Ashkelon—
Broad emblems of our power, that higher came
In martial splendor, homeward turn in shame."

And Achish said, "Once age was reckoned wise,
And skilled to guide each martial enterprise,
Though weak in bone and body. Now the fool
Must have his will, and witless youth will rule
Or else he rages. Be it as ye wish:
But I did battle with the son of Kish
Ere ye were swaddled, and I know the power
That lurks behind his thrust; for since the hour

When Marna dashed the Titans from the door
Of Heaven, was none among the sons of War
Like Saul of Israel. And ye now rebel
Against your captain, when the breath of Hell
Is hot against our faces, and the jaws
Of Death spring wide—ye mock Philistia's laws
And flaunt your folly. David is my helm
And my right arm, the guardian of my realm,
My son and my sustainer, free from guile
Or taint of treason; yet to reconcile
Your childish humors—though his single blade
Is worth an hundred chariots arrayed
For battle, yoked and manned—I bid him go
Unto his city. Let the trumpets blow,
And get you to your posts. And when the spears
Break on our front of battle, and your ears
Are dinned with furious shouting; when ye feel
On gorget and on helm the shock of steel
That sucks the hot blood from you; when the horse
And chariot roll in ruin; may remorse
Devour your hearts." Then wroth but overawed
The princes turned their chariots, and the broad
Hot plain of Kishon smoked beneath the heels
Of snorting steeds, and swiftly rolling wheels
Made earth to tremble: so they reached their post
And quieted the turmoil; and the host
Began to move.

            Then Achish called the son
Of Jesse, saying, "By that Mighty One
Ye worship—for I hold that He is King
Of all the gods—I find no evil thing
Within thine hand: yea, over all mine host
I give thee honor to the uttermost,
And love thy company; but, lest I earn
The anger of Philistia's lords, return

GILBOA

And go in peace. Good art thou in my sight
As Michael the archangel; but thy might
Shall not avail me when the spears of Saul
Come up against me, and his arrows fall
Like hail upon our bucklers. Keep the gate
Of Ziklag from the desert rovers' hate,
And guard my borderlands. And if it chance
I come to grief on Israelitish lance,
Then strike thy zither softly, and lament
The fortune of thy friend. My testament
Is with my steward: I have named thee heir
To my dominions, and thy head shall wear
The diadem of Gath. Behold, my seal
Shall be thy warrant: thou shalt set thine heel
On them that hate thee, and shalt break the teeth
Of all thine enemies. The victor's wreath
Be thine for evermore." And, having said,
He shouted to his steeds; the chariot sped
After the host; and David heard the roar
Recede, and watched the glittering tide of war
Move on and ever on, and shrink in size—
Men, chariots and horses—till his eyes
Could barely see, far off, the shifting shine
Of sun flashed back from spear and brigandine.

Then David called the Priest Abiathar,
And said, "Behold, Jehovah's hand doth mar
The plan that we without his aid devised:
For we have joined with the uncircumcised
Against the peace of Israel, and were hired
As Balaam was of Balak, nor inquired
For counsel at His mouth. We have transgressed
In this against the Lord. But let the rest
Be as He wills. Inquire thou of the Lord
If we shall turn again and sheathe the sword,
Or seek my Lord the King, and proffer aid
Against Philistia's host with spear and blade."

So built the priest an altar to the Lord,
And sacrificed a lamb thereon, and poured
The blood upon the ground, and did entreat
The face of God. And when he heard, he beat
His breast in anguish: "Thus the Lord hath said,
'What mean ye now, ye rebels, that ye tread
My chosen land in arms? Gave I not charge
That thou shouldest draw no weapon, lift no targe
Against the King of Israel? It was I
That made him King; and will ye now defy
The purpose that I purposed, when I poured
The oil upon him, girt him with the sword
Of Israel's strength? I gave him throne and crown
And scepter: I will also cast him down
And rend his realm, because he disobeyed
Mine ordinance. But thou shalt draw no blade
For Saul, nor yet against him. I fill full
His cup of fury: who shall disannul
The thing that I decree, or build again
What I destroy? Among the ways of men
I move unseen of man: the high of soul
Are mine to overthrow, and I will roll
Their glory in the dust. Therefore, return
Unto thy city. Amalek's warriors burn
Thy gates and roofs with fire, and take as prize
Thy wives; and all the pleasure of thine eyes
Is made their booty.' "

                Here the oracle
Grew silent, and the son of Jesse fell
Upon his face and wept, and all his men
Lamented; but God answered not again
For all their supplications.

                And afar
Philistia ranked her chariots of war
Along the vale of Jezreel, whence the ground
Sloped up to high Gilboa, toward the bound

GILBOA

And limit of Manasseh; and the guards
Were posted, and the sentries kept their wards
In either camp; and so the sun went down
Toward Sharon, and the night in sable gown
Came up and took the world.

              And at the last
Did David rise, with all his band, and passed
Through Esdraëlon's darkened plain, and clomb
Megiddo's pass, and took their way toward home
Through Sharon and Philistia. Night and day
They marched, nor scarcely rested by the way,
And came to Ziklag by the desert's edge—
A place of ruin, smitten by the sledge
Of Amalek. The torch and sword had done
Their work of fury; and the desert sun
Looked down on smouldering ruins, where the fire
Yet burnt the places dear to their desire
In happier days; nor any life was there,
Nor any voice to answer their despair.

IV

So the maids of Issachar
    Told the story long ago,
Underneath the evening star;
    So they sang of Israel's woe,
Sang in bitterness and weeping,
With their timbrels measure keeping,
How Philistia's host came sweeping
Up the Kishon's reedy marges,
With their spears and swords and targes
    And their chariots ranked for war.

So it was they told the tale,
    With their garments rent and marred,
Loud lament and bitter wail
    Raised for Saul, the evil-starred:

GILBOA

Saul, who sought the necromancer
When the prophets gave no answer,
Vainly sought from her to borrow
Hope and solace for the morrow;
But he came again in sorrow
   When the morning light grew pale.

Saul the King of Israel seeks
   Counsel for his warring.
Night is on the mountain-peaks;
There is pallor on his cheeks,
   In his soul abhorring.

Saul the King is gray and old,
   Bent with age and sadness.
Though he once was strong and bold,
Hope is faint, and courage cold:
   In his brain is madness.

Abner, Captain of the host,
   Follows, gray with terror;
Jethir, he that loves him most,
Comes behind him like a ghost,
   Friend and armor-bearer.

Saul is garbed in rustic guise,
   Chancing no betrayment,
And his followers go in wise
Meet to cheat too curious eyes,
   Dressed in shepherd's raiment.

They have left their camp behind,
   Down the slope descending;
Gropingly the way they find:
All the path is black and blind,
   Into darkness blending.

GILBOA

Shadowlike they cross the vale
   Where their foes lie sleeping
(So the damsels tell the tale),
Past the sentinels in mail
   Careless vigil keeping.

Wrapped in stillness lies the camp,
   Hushed is each battalion;
Nothing stirs along the ramp,
Save the restless snort and stamp
   Of a wakeful stallion.

Stealthy move the three along,
   Wordless, scarcely breathing.
(So the damsels sing the song.)
All around them dangers throng,
   And their blood is seething.

If their tread a stick shall break,
   Or stone dislodged betray them,
Swift the camp will spring awake,
All around shall weapons shake,
   And the sword shall slay them.

Once the King had called his band,
   In his days of glory,
Blown the trumpet, drawn the brand,
Hewn them down on every hand,
Won such triumph that the land
   Shouted forth the story.

Now he passes like a ghost,
   Seeking for a charmer,
With the Captain of his host,
And the friend who loves him most,
   Bearer of his armor.

GILBOA

Once the King was strong and brave;
   Now his hair is hoary.
Once his hand had might to save,
Help and hope Jehovah gave—
Now he trembles: let the grave
   Hide his tarnished glory.

They have left the tents behind
   Where their foemen slumber;
Now the onward way they find
Through the darkness—soul and mind
   Lost in shades of umber.

On and ever on they fare,
   Abner, Saul, and Jethir,
Shivering in the mountain air,
Heavy-footed with despair,
   Three old men together.

Long ago it was, a lad
   Sought for straying asses,
When the world was young and glad
And the light of wonder clad
   Cobweb-tented grasses.

Memories long in ashes laid:
   Hour of peace and splendor;
Sinking sun; a star-eyed maid
Standing in the olive's shade,
   Radiant and slender....

Memory of that wondrous morn—
   How the dawn came slowly;
Warbling bird and fragrant thorn,
And the Prophet, with his horn
   Filled with unction holy....

GILBOA

 Strange such thoughts came slipping back,
  Flung their glamour o'er him,
 Now, when anguish, like a rack,
 Crushed his spirit, and this black
  Errand lay before him!

 Yea, the two had been his bane,
  Prophet, star-eyed maiden—
 These, that should have blessed his reign,
 Had but brought him grief and pain,
 Left him with a maddened brain,
  Sick and horror-laden.

 So it is the gifts of bliss,
  Love and peace and wonder,
 When profaned or used amiss,
 Batlike flit through Hell's abyss,
  Driven by shafts of thunder.

 On he stumbles, faint and blind,
  Prey to somber musings:
 Wrack and ruin stretch behind;
 Gibbering phantoms in his mind
  Rise with dark accusings.

 So they reach the witch's hut
  In its dewy garden:
 Olive, vine, and almond-nut
 Blackened seem with sorcery's smut;
 All the place from mercy shut,
  Lost to peace or pardon.

 All in breathless hush is bound:
  Breath nor leaf is stirring;
 Nothing breaks the lull profound
 Save a bat that flits around
  And a cricket's chirring.

Jethir's hand is on the latch,
    Abner's shakes the grating.
Silence still: their breath they catch;
Underneath the mouldered thatch
    Shame and doom are waiting....

Then, a sound upon the floor,
    Scrape of foot or sandal;
Doubtful sighs, a creaking door—
And the sorceress stands before,
    With a flickering candle.

This is she thou lovest, Saul:
    Stand, and gaze upon her;
Her, thy sorrow and thy fall;
Her, for whom thou gavest all—
    Faith and truth and honor!

They for this have journeyed far:
    Now their tale hath ending.
Wandering star with wandering star
Meet amidst the gloom of war
    Ere to dark descending.

O'er them wheels the midnight sky,
    Bats around them hover;
Sunken eye meets sunken eye,
Neither knowing other. Why
Meet they thus before they die,
    Atarah, and her lover?

V

So came the King to Atarah by night,
  And knew her not, and said,
"Divine to me by thy familiar sprite:
  Ask counsel of the dead."

She answered him, "My lord, they speak not truth
  Who call me sorceress;
For I have followed virtue from my youth,
  And never did transgress

"Jehovah's statutes, nor the King's command.
  And thou dost know full well
How Saul hath cut the wizards from the land,
  And all that cast a spell

"Or traffic in enchantments. Wherefore set
  A snare for such as I—
A friendless woman? Wilt thou spread a net
  To cause my soul to die?"

The King made answer, "We are from the tent
  Of Saul, and sent by him.
God gives the King no answer, and hath sent
  Upon him terrors grim.

"Now therefore, if thou knowest charm or spell,
  In kindness or for hire
Call up the spirit I shall name from Hell
  To show him his desire.

"And by His name, who moves the stars and hath
  The keys of night and morn,
To thee shall come no punishment or scath:
  So Saul himself hath sworn.

"But if thou wilt not use thy charms to bring
   A counselor from the tomb,
Like one that gropes in darkness shall the King
   Go forth to meet his doom."

She answered softly, "Is it then for Saul
   Ye bid me scan the scroll
Of darkness? In his service, I will call
   The curse upon my soul.

"What matter? For Jehovah's awful eye
   Hath looked upon my guilt:
If I may serve the King before I die,
   I summon whom thou wilt.

"Already, by old sorceries weighted down,
   I sink in marsh and mire.
I sin once more to save my lover's crown
   And give him his desire.

"For I have loved him, long and long ago,
   And still I love his name.
Let Saul be victor when the trumpets blow,
   And I will bear the shame."

She spake beneath her breath: the King half heard,
   Nor heeded what she said,
But waited, hearkening for the dreadful word
   That summoned forth the dead,

And, vexed because the sorceress mumbled so
   And stayed his enterprise,
He marked not how her eyes began to glow
   Like stars in April skies,

GILBOA

While still she murmured on, "My lords, my lords,
   I loved him, knew his kiss!
Our troth was plighted—then came Agag's swords,
   And I am brought to this:

"A poor old woman, outcast and alone,
   Remembering naught but wrong—"
The King spake harshly: "Make the future known.
   We tarry overlong."

And Atarah, grieving like a child in fault,
   That deems itself reproved
Unjustly, yet restrains the drops of salt
   And strives to seem unmoved,

And thinking, "Saul is made of gentler stuff,
   And kind in everything,
But these his messengers are warriors rough—
   They are not like the King;

"Yet must I do them service for his sake,
   Must put repentance by
And speak the incantation, though I break
   The Lord's command, and die;"

She crossed the room, and lit three lamps of oil
   To charm the evil powers,
Breathed on the brazier, set a pot to boil
   With herbs and withered flowers;

And asked of Saul, "Whom would ye that I bring?
   For now ye see the spell
Is ready." And with pallid lips the King
   Made answer, "Samuel."

She muttered words unlawful to be writ,
    Her eyes upon the ground
In dreadful expectation; and the pit
    Opened without a sound,

And one like Samuel rose, with angry look
    And smelling of the tomb:
The lamplight flickered, and the hard earth shook,
    And whispers filled the room.

Then Atarah gave one lamentable cry
    That shook her withered frame:
"Thou art the King! Now therefore let me die,
    For thou hast seen my shame!"

But Saul, who deemed her fearful of his wrath,
    Replied, "Put by thy fears:
Thou hast mine oath that none shall do thee scath.
    Who is he that appears?"

She answered shuddering, "Dreadful as a god
    From Tartarus evoked,
He stands, graybearded, reeking of the clod,
    In prophet's mantle cloaked."

So Saul discerned the Prophet, though the place
    Was empty to his sense
Of vision; and he bowed upon his face
    And did him reverence.

Then came a hollow voice, that pricked the hair,
    Though naught was manifest
But curling vapor in the empty air:
    "Why breakest thou my rest?"

GILBOA

And Saul replied, "Because I am undone.
   Philistia hems me in
With spears and chariots; and the Holy One
   Regardeth yet my sin

"And will accord no answer to my prayer
   By dream or prophet's word,
And I am left in anguish and despair,
   Forsaken of the Lord.

"And I have sought thee out, who long ago
   Wast counselor and friend
To me, before my follies brought me low,
   That I may know mine end."

Then spake the voice, "And wherefore dost thou call
   On me, since God hath done
According to my word, and given all
   Thy realm to Jesse's son?

"There is no help; for God hath done this thing:
   He hath arrayed the spears
Against thy kingdom, and His hand shall bring
   The thunders in thine ears

"To cast thee down to ruin. It is He
   That overthrows thine hosts:
To-morrow thou and they shall be with me
   Among the bloodless ghosts."

He ceased: and Saul cried out, and fell full length,
   His face upon the ground,
Like one whom terror hath deprived of strength,
   And lay without a sound.

The sorceress hasted, with soft, clucking cries,
   And lifted up his head,
Above him bending with her piteous eyes:
   "Ah God! He is not dead!

"It cannot be that he is dead so soon,
   The majesty and pride
Of Israel! Oh then, let sun and moon
   In night their radiance hide!"

And Abner said, "He is not dead, good dame,
   But only faint with fear
And fasting. Though it flickers like a flame,
   The spirit still is here."

Then rose the King, and said, "Though I be cursed
   Of God, and tumbled low,
I will not tremble, since I know the worst:
   I will abide the blow.

"And when my kingdom sinks in blood and night
   And David takes the crown,
Make known to him it was no mortal might
   But God that cast me down."

Then Atarah besought him, "O my lord,
   Let bread and ruddy wine
Refresh thy soul, before thou gird the sword
   To smite the Philistine."

He answered, "Nay, I will not rest nor eat.
   The hour is hard at hand
Of desolation: kinglike let me meet
   The ruin of my land."

But Abner and his servant pressed him sore:
"The woman speaketh well.
Now therefore eat and rest thyself, before
Thou strike for Israel."

Constrained by them, he sat upon the bed,
And mused upon his doom,
While Atarah dressed a calf and kneaded bread,
Bustling about the room.

The hour was come that she had dreamed so oft
In those far days and fair
When hope was like a lark that soared aloft
Unshadowed by despair:

The hour to do him service with her hands,
Of which the birds had sung
When winds blew softly over April lands,
And both of them were young.

And now they both were old and stained with sin,
The hopes of youth were past;
And lo, this hallowed hour, that should have been
Long since, was come at last!

She sod the flesh and set the dough to bake,
With soft eyes fixed upon
The troubled King, half fearing she should wake
And find the vision gone.

This hour her girlhood hopes had burst in bloom:
She breathed their hallowed air.
She would remember, to the trump of doom,
Their joy and their despair.

She served her guests with hands that scarce could hold
    The wine-cup and the food;
By turns her cheeks were pale and icy cold
    Or hot with throbbing blood.

For still her fingers ached to touch his cheek
    Or hair; and all the while
She dumbly prayed, "Ah God, will he not speak?
    Ah God, will he not smile?"

Saul neither spake nor smiled, but like a beast
    Devoured the meal in haste;
For soon would come a pallor in the east:
    Scant time was left to waste.

He drained his cup, and suddenly arose:
    "We must depart with speed.
The night grows short; the way is thick with foes.
    Give to the witch her meed."

He spake, and turned away. A piece of gold
    Flashed in the candle-light:
On Atarah's cheek the garden air blew cold:
    They vanished into night,

Three gray old men, like figures in a dream,
    Whose shadows went before
Across the garden, where the candle's gleam
    Fell from the open door.

A while she harked to their receding tramp
    Across the stony ground;
A cricket chattered where the dew lay damp:
    There came no other sound.

GILBOA

And Atarah uttered one despairing cry
   And sank upon the floor:
"Mine eyes have seen him; therefore let me die!
   I shall not see him more.

"And it was through my sorcery he heard
   His doom—and he is gone.
He gave me gold, but spake no kindly word...
   How is it I live on?

"I had not thought that he would be so old,
   So gaunt, so bowed with care.
How black has grown the darkness... and how cold...
   Where is the candle?... Where?"

So ends the scene: the golden hour is done,
   And Fate hath had her will.
The lamps burn down to darkness, one by one:
   The sorceress lies still.

And Saul the King goes plodding through the night,
   With hopeless anguish dumb;
And as he climbs Gilboa's rugged height
   Gray dawn begins to come.

VI

It is morning in the mountains, and Philistia's camp
      hath stirred,
   And the blood of men is singing like the singing
      of a bird.
   Now has dawned the day of battle, and the mailed
      battalions form—
   There is flash of furbished lances like the lightnings
      of the storm.

GILBOA

Hanun mounts his gilded chariot, with his trumpet
    at his mouth:
(David and his men are marching through the desert
    of the South.)

Rusa buckles harness on him, Adimar hath girt the
    blade;
There is shout and snort and trample, and Philistia
    stands arrayed.
Now the ranks are moving onward, o'er the stream
    and up the steep,
Where the bands of Israel huddle like a flock of
    frightened sheep,
While the trumpets shout their challenge and the
    chariots shake the earth—
(In the house of Saul at Gibeah, Rizpah travaileth
    in birth.)

Shining like the rays of morning, onward still the
    lances come,
And the rugged slopes are shaken with the rumble
    of the drum.
Chariot and horse rush forward, driven by the
    cracking whips,
Tossing like the sea in tempest, when he swallows
    down the ships;
Regal flags like birds are flying high above the
    froth of war—
(Atarah the witch lies dying in her chamber at
    En-dor.)

Israel's host for war is marshaled: Abner leads the
    eastern wing;
Jonathan the leftward legions; in the center stands
    the King;

GILBOA

Adriel's post is in the vanguard, where the
    sharpened stakes are set,
And the stones are heaped for rolling all along the
    parapet;
Phaltiel commands the rearguard, but his face is
    gray with fear,
And he hears the roar and rumble, and he holds not
    glory dear.

Who hath strength to stand against her, when
    Philistia's chariots roll?
Let him arm himself with thunders, praying God to
    keep his soul!
Who hath valor to withstand her, when her
    drums for battle beat,
And the flinty rock is crumbled into fire beneath
    her feet?
Saul the King beholds the onset— O for David's
    spear and brand!
(David chases Amalek's warriors through the waste
    of thorn and sand.)

Onward sweeps the line of chariots, like a wave
    with foam of steel;
Louder swells the roar of onset, pounding hoof and
    grinding wheel.
They have struck! In froth and thunder on the bank
    the billow breaks:
Horse and chariot and rider thrash among the spears
    and stakes,
While with shout and clash of weapons hand to
    hand the battle joins:
Adriel falls in mortal anguish with a sword-thrust
    through the loins.

Hanun's host are o'er the rampart, and the few
    defenders fly;
Fleet of foot the foemen follow, and their war-shout
    shakes the sky.
Now the bows begin their twanging, and the
    bronze-barbed arrows sing:
Hanun's men have joined the battle with the
    warriors of the King.
Slowly from their thrusting lances Israel's
    hard-pressed troops recoil—
(David smites the desert raiders, and goes
    homeward with the spoil.)

Achish swerves his line of battle, skirting outwork,
    ditch and bank,
And his chariots fall in fury full on Israel's western
    flank,
And the scythes upon the axles mow the spearmen
    down like grain:
Jonathan the Prince is fallen with a sword-cut
    through the brain.
Trodden down beneath the horses, lo, he writhes
    upon the earth—
(Rizpah's breath comes hot and panting: she hath
    brought her sons to birth.)

Adimar hath struck to eastward: Abner's hardy
    courage fails,
For the weapons of Philistia rise and fall like
    threshers' flails;
Flash of helm and gleam of buckler mar the Hebrew
    bowmen's aim,
And the line of battle crumples like a parchment in
    the flame,
Till the craven flee in terror and the valiant roll in
    gore—
(Pale and breathless in her cottage, Atarah lies upon
    the floor.)

GILBOA

VII

The dusk hath fallen on Gilboa's height:
    Drumbeat and trumpet-peal
Are hushed, and all the turmoil of the fight;
    The clang of steel,

The shout and snort and trample—these are done,
    And quiet holds the hill;
For Israel's hosts have fallen one by one,
    And they lie still.

Beside the banks of Acheron, the shades
    Of the old dead make room
For crowding ghosts with dinted shields and blades
    And draggled plume.

All day the fight hath raged upon the slope,
    And Saul, with shattered shield,
Still keeps his place, as one that hath no hope,
    Yet will not yield.

His sons are fallen, yea, and all his house,
    The men that girt his mail,
Lie with the dew of death upon their brows,
    Bloodless and pale.

O'er Saul himself have rolled the floods of war,
    And though he still lives on,
The arrows and the swords have galled him sore,
    And strength is gone.

And with him there is left upon the field
    But one to share his end:
The bondman Jethir, bearer of his shield,
    His boyhood friend;

GILBOA

Two gray-haired men, they lean on blunted brands,
    Comrades through storm and stress;
They gasp for breath: the hilts cleave to their hands
    From weariness.

Then spake the King, "Philistia wins the field;
    My kingdom lies in dust.
I never more shall buckle on the shield:
    The Lord is just,

"For I rebelled against him, and despised
    His counsel, to maintain
My stubborn pride. And these uncircumcised
    Will mock my pain

"If they shall find me. Let it be the end:
    The time is come to part,
And I am ready. Draw thy sword, old friend:
    Strike to the heart."

He answered, "Thou wast chosen of the Lord
    As King; and thou shalt be
My King for ever. Never shall my sword
    Be drawn on thee."

Then Saul drew forth the weapon from his side
    And stood it on the ground
And leaned his breast upon it: so he died
    Without a sound.

Then Jethir, saying, "Now in everything
    Let me fulfill thy will,"
Fell on his sword, and died beside the King,
    And both lay still.

GILBOA

    So fell the King of Israel, and his sons,
       And all that drew the breath
    Of Saul's—the captains and the mighty ones—
       Lay still in death.

    And all the host of heaven went marching past,
       With pitiless pomp and glitter
    Above the dead; and gray dawn broke at last,
       And birds began to twitter.

www.ingramcontent.com/pod-product-compliance
Lightning Source LLC
Chambersburg PA
CBHW021119300426
44113CB00006B/217